A Woman's Guide
to Small Business

A Woman's Guide to Small Business

Hayley Lewis

HarperCollins*Publishers*
harpercollins.com.au

IMPORTANT NOTE

The material presented in this book is for the purpose of general information only. Neither the author nor the publisher in any way warrant or guarantee that the strategies and methods described in this book are suitable for your particular business objectives, financial situation or needs. Before making a financial decision on the basis of any information presented in this book, please seek professional advice from a qualified financial advisor.

HarperCollins*Publishers*

First published in Australia in 2011
by HarperCollins*Publishers* Australia Pty Limited
ABN 36 009 913 517
harpercollins.com.au

Copyright © Hayley Lewis 2011

The right of Hayley Lewis to be identified as the author of this work has been asserted by her under the *Copyright Amendment (Moral Rights) Act 2000*.

HarperCollins*Publishers*
25 Ryde Road, Pymble, Sydney, NSW 2073, Australia
31 View Road, Glenfield, Auckland 0627, New Zealand
A 53, Sector 57, Noida, UP, India
77–85 Fulham Palace Road, London W6 8JB, United Kingdom
2 Bloor Street East, 20th floor, Toronto, Ontario M4W 1A8, Canada
10 East 53rd Street, New York NY 10022, USA

National Library of Australia Cataloguing-in-Publication entry:

Lewis, Hayley.
Dream believe create : a woman's guide to small business / Hayley Lewis.
ISBN: 978 0 7322 9214 0 (pbk.)
Small business – Australia – Management.
Women-owned business enterprises – Australia.
658.0220994

Cover design by Priscilla Nielsen
Cover photography by Erik Williamson; all other images shutterstock.com
Internal design by Alicia Freile, Tango Media
Typeset in Goudy Old Style 10/13pt by Kirby Jones
Printed and bound in Australia by Griffin Press
70gsm Classic used by HarperCollins*Publishers* is a natural, recyclable product made from wood grown in sustainable forests. The manufacturing processes conform to the environmental regulations in the country of origin, Finland.

5 4 3 2 1   11 12 13 14

To the three Taylor boys, Greg, Jacob and Kai

Contents

Everything Starts with a Dream

One of my lifelong dreams has been to write a book and have it published. I've been thinking about it for a while now, but it never seemed like the right time. My hope is that when you spotted this book on the shelf, you became even more inspired to start believing your dreams could possibly come true.

The whole premise of this book is to offer advice in the areas that I am truly experienced in. I don't pretend to have knowledge of absolutely every area of business, nor do I have a degree in business or finance. Instead, I can simply offer to give you the benefit of my business experience and to point you towards the best advice and assistance I can supply. Many business books are penned by authors with degrees in business-related areas, but a proportion haven't actually owned, managed or run their own businesses. I have — and I'd like to share some of my personal stories and business wisdom with you.

Simply choosing to purchase this book means you have now taken the all-important step into the initial 'preparation stage'. Well done! I love meeting female small business owners because I feel we're a revolutionary bunch. We've got the tenacity and get-up-and-go to meet the challenges we set for ourselves. This book is designed specifically for the forward-thinking woman and throughout its pages I'll give you a personal account of life in the small business world, along with some experiences from other female entrepreneurs living their dreams.

Essentially, I've tried to create a comprehensive source of information to help guide women through the initial planning of their business to the days, months and hopefully years of trading ahead. From the first 'idea phase', right through to the 'finishing line', this book attempts to tackle most of the challenges you'll encounter along the way and gives practical advice to inspire you through to the end.

Being your own boss is all about opportunity and commitment. Running your own business certainly has many perks and, to some extent, a lot of freedom to be creative and make your own decisions on a daily basis. How wonderfully amazing is that? However, with this freedom comes a lot of accountability and responsibility. I want you to know that I'm definitely on your side. See me as the faithful and tough coach, Mickey, from the *Rocky* movies. I'm trying to prime you so that you're totally prepared when you begin this crusade.

I have faith in you. Keep this book close at hand. I know you can do it.

Dream Believe Create

Hayley

My Life's Business

From small beginnings

On your marks ...

My own small business

My little tips

From small beginnings

One of my many dreams when I was growing up was to have my very own small business. I remember thinking how wonderful it would be to own a lolly shop or perhaps a doll shop. Actually, I don't think it really mattered what I sold, I just wanted to play 'shopkeeper' in a little corner store that I could operate myself.

As a young girl, I obviously had no comprehension of the long list of responsibilities and costs associated with being self-employed. Thankfully, when I did finally become a small business owner many years later, I still wasn't deterred by the whole notion that my success and longevity in small business hinged on how much effort and time I was willing to put in. Nine years on, I do believe that some people are born to be business owners while others perhaps are not. I have quite a few friends who have no idea why anyone could possibly want to work for themselves, while others could think of nothing worse than having to work for someone else for even a day, let alone their whole working lives. I definitely sit firmly in the latter category and I'm not sure how this came about.

Both my parents are firmly of the mind-set that running your own small business is quite risky. Mum has always been a 'stay at home' mum and Dad has worked at the *Courier Mail* newspaper in Brisbane for 45 years, so branching out and dreaming of becoming an entrepreneur was definitely a gamble in the Lewis household. When I was about 10 years old, my dad bought his own bread delivery business. My only memories of that period were that we seemed to have heaps of money and heaps of bread, but we never really saw our dad because he was either working hard or sleeping. Thankfully, that entrepreneurial phase for my dad only lasted about 12 months before he was back at the paper and we had him back in our lives, albeit with a little less money and a lot less bread! During that time, I realised the sacrifices that families make to run their own small businesses. Dad's bread run was a 24-hour, seven-day-a-week energy-zapper.

For this very reason, I can clearly remember to this day the perplexed and concerned looks on my parents' faces when I told them that I was thinking of starting my own swim school.

'Why would you want to do that? It all sounds like a huge risk and a lot of work if you ask me!' my mum stated with furrowed brow.

'I hope you know what you're doing,' my dad replied, with trepidation creeping across his face. I'm sure the magnitude of sleep deprivation from his own small business days had scarred him mentally for life.

I considered for a second or two the 'question/remark' phase of the parental discussion, before deciding quite quickly that as much as I loved my parents, this new adventure I was about to undertake would not be easy for them to understand or feel relaxed about. For me, their reactions of ambivalence and worry were only bolstering my determination to succeed and forge ahead with my plans. I knew within myself that starting my own business would fulfil a lifelong dream — one that would be both rewarding and challenging — and no one was going to deter me, especially my well-meaning parents. That being said, I really didn't comprehend exactly what I was getting myself into either. I had exactly zero hours of experience in *any* business, let alone creating and managing one for myself. I'm certainly not one to waste time pondering the what-ifs, so I dived right in ... so to speak.

Looking back at the past nine years of being self-employed, there are certainly days when I felt like packing it all in, but it has never, nor will it *ever* be an option to go and work for someone else. It's not that I don't like people — in fact I'm pro-people — but I think I just don't like people telling me what to do. I know this sentiment is without doubt the result of my many years as a competitive swimmer. From the age of four through to 27 I was dictated to by programs, swimming carnivals, coaches, diets, exercise regimens, early bedtimes, you name it! As an athlete, I had to be 100 per cent disciplined about every aspect of my life, otherwise it would have been a complete waste of time and effort. It was very much a regimented schedule that I can't believe I maintained for so many years without going crazy. In saying this, I know it made me toughen up and not be complacent to go through life looking for a challenge or two. At 37 and a mum of two, I can finally cherish the fact that I can now live life to the beat of my own drum and not someone else's.

If you are anything like I was prior to starting out on my own, then you're probably spending many sleepless nights just fantasising about owning your own small business, but may not quite know where to begin. Let me be upfront by admitting that even with nine years of small business experience behind me, I would certainly change many decisions I made along the way. The initial stages were far from perfect, but I started with a modest base and built on it. While admitting this, I can at least pass on some helpful and timesaving tips I managed to pick up along the way and these might help to alleviate some of your pre-business angst.

By entering the world of the entrepreneur you are in fact demonstrating that you are quite the idealist. To have the aspiration and motivation to start planning a new business venture takes courage and an innovative spirit. There are thousands of women every year that dream of 'going it alone' and sadly many of these fall by the wayside. Make sure you do everything in your power to be one of those that goes the distance.

Having been in business for many years now I've remained happy, committed and not at all jaded by the whole experience. This has allowed me to understand how special it is to be a successful small business operator in shaky and uncertain financial times.

My job also allows wonderful opportunities to meet and communicate with many different women from all walks of life on a daily basis. Surprisingly, they all seem to have more in common than just being female. Quite a large percentage seems to work part-time or full-time jobs, with many saying they don't particular enjoy what they do but are simply working out of necessity. Many also admit quite openly that they just want to get out of the house and spend some time around other adults, while having the obvious added benefit of earning their own money. Whatever the reason or motivation, most women are active and industrious characters by nature, so to have the desire to wear a variety of hats during a lifetime is purely part of our genetic make-up.

It's really no great surprise either that as organised and hard-working females, we all feel that magnetic pull to be creative and passionate about things outside the confines of our homes. Considering the percentage of women entering the workforce each year, not to mention the recent statistics indicating that one third of small business operators are women, there is a clear demonstration that trends within the workplace are changing. The world is evolving and as women we are calling upon our resourcefulness to become not only income contributors but in many cases the primary breadwinners within the family. I believe that as a result of this positive female phenomenon, men are becoming more comfortable with successful women in the workplace.

And why shouldn't this be the case? We're not going to work because we have nothing else to do with our time. Some of us are actually bringing home quite an impressive pay packet. This is by no means an opportunity for me to attack the guys out there either, but purely an opportunity to state the obvious revolution of the 21st century. Anyway, why shouldn't men be OK with women adding to the financial strength of the household? As my husband has aptly commented at certain moments during our marriage: 'Happy wife, happy life'. These days women feel inspired and eager to work, so simply giving us the opportunity and support to do so will not only increase our confidence but also make us content with life in general. By giving women the support we deserve, I guarantee that the household will be a more peaceful environment for everyone to share. I'll let you in on a secret: women are not anywhere near as complicated as men seem to think. We just need to love what we do, have people around us who think we are amazing and every now and again have the opportunity to get a massage and not feel incredibly guilty about it. Simple!

Coincidentally, at my little swim school in Brisbane I have a noticeboard for parents wishing to tack up notices and advertisements for their businesses. Some are even massage businesses — what an ironic twist! All the advertisements are for wonderfully creative and innovative products and services, but after a period of time the notices are pulled down by the owner and discarded sheepishly because of a lack of interest from potential customers. I think many of us are itching to get that 'one big break', but we forget that the most important aspects of being successful are planning, perseverance and patience. Unfortunately, it's not that uncommon to witness the success stories of other women, and before you know it, they're on *Oprah* boasting about their successes and triumphs. If you're anything like me, then you're most probably berating the television and screaming out: 'I could have done that. I had that idea a year ago!'

Ninety-eight per cent of success is isolating an opportunity — and that's exactly what those women on *Oprah* have done. They recognised a gap, built a concept and challenged themselves. These women are no different to you and me. In fact, by flicking through these pages, chances are you have already noticed an opportunity and are in the research phase at this very moment. You are currently committing yourself to a personal dream that requires a lot of planning before anything else. Take it from me, one of the world's most impatient people, it will serve you well to carry out thorough research and comprehensively prepare yourself before jumping into the deep end. Leave nothing to chance in this preparatory stage. I did everything within my power not to cut corners at this crucial phase, but with hindsight, I can see that because I had a particular deadline to meet — that is, an opening date — some areas were rushed instead of being given the focus they deserved. If being a little more meticulous with your research results in a later starting date than you had initially wished for, then you should view it as a blessing and not a major backward step for the business. I am a firm believer in the phrase 'everything happens for a reason' and if you find yourself being hit by setback after setback, eventually you will see a positive reason behind it, hopefully.

Many of the business-related books I've read were extremely helpful and I still return to them for ideas. Sadly, not many of these are from a female perspective, which was my original inspiration to put pen to paper. It's my opinion that women think differently and more from the heart than men do, and I believe it can be helpful to have guidance from a person of the same sex. In a way, it makes you have a sense of *Well, if she did it, then I might be able to do it too!* I think we're often tougher than some men give us credit for — either that, or we keep it very well hidden. Whatever the reason, I feel there is something about female intuition that bestows an uncanny knack for knowing when something is a good idea or when it's a fizzer.

When I first went to my manager with the idea for this book, he was very sceptical.

'Do you write much?' he asked, with doubt and cynicism lashing his tone.

'Well, I don't write books as a hobby in my spare time, but I love to read; the only subject I was good at school was English; I have my own business that I started from scratch; plus I've already written the first three chapters for you to have a look at. If you think that I'm not very good, then at least I haven't wasted much of my time thinking I was a great writer when I really wasn't.'

My manager's lack of enthusiasm, as well as his uncertainty about my writing ability, annoyed me a little because it reminded me of his reaction when I told him that I wanted to be considered for the new hosting role on *The Biggest Loser*.

'You've never been interested in being on television ... *ever!*' he commented with a confused and almost incredulous tone.

'Just put my name in the mix and what will be will be,' I said, thinking to myself that never in a million years would I even be considered anyway.

I have known my manager for a long time and I know he has faith in me, but when someone shows a hint of doubt in my abilities, it's like adding fuel to the competitive fire that burns within me. Well, something strange and wonderful happened and I ended up with the hosting job, which in turn has changed my manager's perception of what I'm able to do.

So, that's how this book came about. During the writing process, I realised how much I still love being a small business owner and how proud I am of creating my little service to the community. Sometimes as a business owner the time rushes by too quickly for you to have the opportunity to be proud of what you have created. Maybe after those first few hectic years, you will find the perfect time to reflect on your wonderful creation.

My swim school is by no means a massive establishment. In fact, it's quite 'boutique' in nature, taking up an area of 15 by 6 metres. Some families brought their babies to my swim school nine years ago and now those babies are in Grade Three at school and still swimming at my centre — how special is that? The loyalty of those families is not lost on me. I'm extremely honoured they remained steadfast, even when larger, more impressive swim schools were being built like fortresses around me. I hope when you build your own business, be it small or large, that you will enjoy both the good days and the not so great ones. Some days will be tough, but you will gain a lot more knowledge from those days than from the easier ones. Either way, you are about to embark on what could be a very positive, life-altering journey, and by putting yourself out there and having a go, you have already taken a positive step towards a new life for yourself. Just remember to keep your head a fraction below the clouds in order to remain focused on the task at hand. The worst thing to do at this stage is to allow yourself to get too caught up in the excitement of what could possibly be a remarkably rewarding career. Remain positive and confident but never brash or arrogant. It will never serve you well to boast about anything in life (one of my mother's lifelong tips). Even when you become a business mogul and you end up in *BRW* for your amazing conquests, always remember where you started out — at the bottom just plugging along and hoping for a little success.

On your marks ...

Here are a few questions to think about before *BRW* starts calling:

- What makes your business idea unique?
- Is the marketplace saturated with similar concepts?
- Is it economically viable for you?
- Do you have the skills and experience to back up your business idea?
- Are you self-motivated and committed?
- Do you have the capital/cash flow required to start a business?
- Do you feel you have the personal attributes to be your own boss?

I ask these questions because that's what my husband asked me when I boldly informed him that I wanted to start my own business. I remember feeling really angry that he'd been so blunt and straightforward with me. The people that love and care for you will probably ask similar questions, so make sure you are well prepared with some great replies.

Don't take it personally. I'm glad that I was asked those questions. It really did make me think about whether I was completely ready to take on such an immense commitment. You *do* want to make sure that your idea to be a small business owner is not just a flippant whim brought on because you're sick of your day job or you're simply tired of having a boss to answer to. Being a small business owner is one of life's biggest responsibilities — it demands and requires unwavering perseverance and dedication.

Throughout this book, I may ask you some tough questions from time to time, but it's only to get your business mind engaged in thinking through the various situations that crop up on a daily basis in the world of small business. Just remember, I'm on your side. I want nothing more than to see another female small business owner go on to be a shining star in the community. However, I don't want to see another 'sister' start a small business only to see the doors close a premature and disappointing six months down the track. My main focus and priority is to coach and prepare you for a successful road ahead.

I will also be concentrating on motivating you as much as possible, while still reminding you to keep a realistic approach to your business expectations and goals. Far too many budding entrepreneurs become overwhelmed and then disheartened even before the door of their business opens. You have to keep in the forefront of your mind that this whole start-up phase can cause even more pressure and stress than the actually daily running of the business itself. If by the end of this book I have given you the impression that starting a small business is hard work and that it will involve a lot of well-thought-out exploration and planning, then I will have achieved my main objective — I'll be very satisfied. If I've turned you off becoming an entrepreneur all together — well, *excellent*! I've probably saved you thousands of dollars, countless tears and a lot of heartache (although part of me will also feel extremely guilty for doing so). If I've managed to light a fire even brighter in your belly, then I certainly give you kudos for your self-belief and desire. Basically, I want you to realise that *anything is possible*, but you don't want to start trading only to find yourself looking in the Careers section for a job in six months because you didn't plan thoroughly.

I hope I'll have you considering issues that you may not have considered or thought were not necessarily important or instrumental in getting your business off the ground. Anyone can start a business, but the fact is it takes something special to keep the doors open and the money flowing in. There are certainly some very successful business people in the community who have gone on to conquer the small business world yet they started out with no outside assistance or financial support. Remember, you can't cross the ocean without losing sight of the shore. A business is much more than a job — it's a 24/7 commitment that requires 100 per cent of your attention. The more information there is for aspiring female entrepreneurs, the more success and happiness will follow.

My own small business

To this very day, I still visualise my ultimate small business dream — a yarn and homewares store with a quaint and intimate coffee shop attached. I know this sounds completely out of left field for an ex-athlete and television host, but we all have our dreams. It must be a female thing anyway, because many women I have mentioned my dream to seem to love the coffee-shop-attached-to-something idea as well. Don't get me wrong — owning my swim school has been extremely rewarding, but if I'm honest, I'm the girl who loves everything a bit dreamy and whimsical and I've always wanted a little store of my own of some description.

Plus, I'm quite certain, given the nasal sound of my voice, that my sinuses have been completely obliterated by the chlorine I've inhaled over the past 37 years, and I think I deserve some relief from the constant bombardment.

So why did I open a swim school and not my ultimate dream store? Well, there are actually two very good reasons for this. The first is that there would have been absolutely no hope in the world that I could have convinced my husband that opening a corner store was a viable means of paying off our mortgage, *and* I was too scared to dive into something other than a pool or anything that wasn't swimming-related — literally! Besides, I was 28 and had never known much more than the inside of swimming complexes, so it seemed a natural progression for me. It was also an easy sell to both my husband and the bank's loan officer. It does seem strange when I confront the reality that I own a successful swim school and yet I have never felt compelled to own more than one centre, even when it was almost offered to me on a silver platter. I guess I always felt I would be tempting fate to expand, plus life throws certain curve-balls at you that are very unexpected and stressful. I've somehow managed to operate the swim school through the birth of my second child, the sudden death of my beautiful sister, my mum's cancer and then of course landing a television job that required me to spend half the year in another state. Thankfully, I hadn't expanded beyond what I could cope with, mentally and physically.

I spent years procrastinating and dreaming about what I'd love to do for a career before starting the swim school instead of actually putting the preparation and planning into motion. When I'd think about what it would be like to own my own business, I'd always get to the point where it all just seemed too hard. Unfortunately, as an aspiring business owner you learn quickly that no one is going to serve this up on a stress-free platter for you, so that's when you take a big breath and get things moving along yourself, trying not to let any negative thoughts enter your mind. Things may often get to the stage where it all seems *way* too hard to continue. Just remember that there are certainly no guarantees that things will pan out the way you hope or imagine in the real world of small business, especially if you allow negative thoughts to get the better of you.

Having the desire to start your own business is popular among women of all ages, but seeing that idea become a reality is an entirely more complicated and laborious thing. After all, many of us as young girls had lemonade stands outside our childhood homes attempting to make a few dollars. I know I did! I can still picture myself standing outside the front of our suburban Brisbane home with my little fold-out chair under the beach umbrella selling my cool summer drinks to anyone that cared to stop — and I'm quite certain no one actually did. Fast forward 30 years and it certainly conjures up unrealistic images of what a genuine small business is all about. As a young girl, I remember speaking openly about my potential empires to anyone who would listen and it was only when I grew up that I realised there was a lot more to this 'business thing' than I'd first thought. I believe most women have the ability to turn their dreams into reality — after all, we have a great work ethic and loads of determination to back it up. Sometimes we just need a little nudge in the right direction to get us started.

When I first started doing the research for my own small business in 2001, I bought every business book that was written. Let's face it — I had to! I had never even *had* a job, let alone know how to start one from scratch. I have since had the opportunity to reflect on this odd situation and I still don't know if it was a positive or negative for me. I went into everything with absolutely no on-the-job experience, but I was very well equipped and confident that I had the knowledge base for my proposed business idea. Unfortunately, having the knowledge base of a swimmer didn't equate into knowing how to run a small business. In fact, I was like an expectant mother waiting for her first baby when I was preparing to start trading. I had hundreds of well-meaning people offering all types of advice that seemed both helpful and hindering, but secretly I thought *this will be great and easy and I'll be the best business owner the world has ever seen*. It's only now that I realise how naïve and delusional I was before I started trading. It didn't even occur to me to be a little worried that I had outlaid quite a substantial amount of money in order to give myself a career. I either had a disjointed belief in myself that everything would work out fine and dandy, or I had absolutely no idea what lay ahead of me. I tend to think it was a smattering of both.

Looking back to the pre-opening days, I really did believe in myself 100 per cent. I also had an unwavering sense that my business brainwave was a great idea and there was absolutely nil chance of failing. Belief in yourself is an essential quality for those treading the often rocky and treacherous path into small business. There is absolutely no room for self-doubt once you start this journey. Certainly, you can allow for the odd moment or two when spanners get thrown into the works, but you must remain focused and determined not to let issues mess with your ultimate goals. Don't allow yourself to think that your idea isn't worth researching or investigating. How can anyone's ideas be a waste of time without first giving it a chance to fly? Just focus on collecting the information necessary to feel confident that your dream is tangible. This way, the naysayers won't be able to break through your iron-clad, self-assured wall of positivity that you have built up inside you. You'll have concise and confident answers for those who question aspects of your idea. For example, I knew for a fact that my parents were concerned that I was biting off more than I could chew. At every opportunity they would start off their questions with 'Have you thought about x, y and z?'

'Actually, yes I have, as a matter of fact, and here is my well-researched and thoroughly thought-out answer to keep your worries and concerns at bay ... blah, blah, blah,' I would reply with confidence and a tiny little bit of smugness.

My advice is to dot your i's and cross your t's, and you'll be just fine — *plus* you'll give yourself a greater grasp of the business background and reassurance that you have covered all areas before you take the plunge.

During the early days I remember feeling like such an independent woman, with a self-belief that made me either totally indestructible or incredibly naïve. Owning a small business is like being on a roller coaster — there will be days when things couldn't go more wrong and other days when you think things couldn't get any better. This is part and parcel of business and we all experience it. Remember you are creating something out of nothing and now it is time to make the most of the opportunity you have created for yourself: A NEW LIFE!

So, where do I go from here? I've never thought about expanding or franchising my swim school and maybe this has been the wrong move for me financially, who knows? I can tell you one thing for certain; I haven't completely forgotten my dream of a little corner store of some description. I would at least be armed with a wealth of experience to understand what running a business is all about. Plus, I think I almost feel ready to embark on a new adventure.

There are a many reasons why some of us definitely shouldn't contemplate starting a business. It might be something as small as 'timing' or something incredibly important such as 'financial pressure'. Weighing up your personal position in life is incredibly important and starting your own business should be viewed in somewhat the same context as having a baby. Both are life-changing, 24/7 responsibilities that come with definite financial pressures. Be sure you do an honest pros-and-cons checklist before you rush into anything. Either way, it will be an interesting journey, full of twists and turns, but it will be a journey no less and one that you can look forward to.

I have learnt in the past that anything is possible if you keep your dream in clear view and stay motivated. Don't ever let anyone stand in front of your dream. If you are currently in the 'dream stage' of envisioning your own small business, then it's time to get brutally honest with yourself before you stray too far into the woods and feel you've wasted valuable time and energy. Small business is not for the faint-hearted. If you are strong of mind and have the desire to create a dream, then the sky's the limit for your new career. However, be prepared for those that may not share the excitement of your new venture. Their reaction or feelings towards your plans may stem from genuine concern for your livelihood or may even harbour a little bit of jealousy. It is important that you realise that this is *your* dream — someone else's reactions shouldn't sway you or make you feel differently towards it.

My little tips

- Don't be put off by hard work.
- Expect the people closest to you to question everything.
- Love what you do and be inspired every day.
- Don't let setbacks get in the way of your dreams.
- Believe in yourself.

Let's Get Started

Your business idea

What is your small business idea? Does it centre on your favourite hobby or perhaps something that brings enjoyment and happiness to your life? Or is it simply a business that you've always been interested in? Whatever the motivation, you've made the first major step towards moving forward with a new self-made career. More importantly, who wouldn't want to wake up each morning knowing that they were going to a job that was challenging and interesting?

Over the past few years I have read many business books and articles that suggest that turning your favourite hobby into a business venture could be fraught with danger. Why? Apparently, it's because it takes something that is usually your stress release (or boredom buster) and weds it to the everyday ho-hum of work. This could be true, but the argument I make as a woman is this: the majority of us have more than one hobby or interest anyway, so why not indulge in one and make a business out of it? I have a long list of other things that could keep me quite entertained and relaxed for the rest of my life. If I were to start a business from just one of these, I would still have a whole bucketful of pastimes to keep me occupied and relaxed in any spare second I could find. I'm quite certain the same could be said for most women out there, but just because I love knitting, should I consider opening up a yarn store? At present, armed with the small business knowledge I have gained over the past nine years, probably not. I've knitted several jumpers and scarves and people tell me that my knitting is great. So, what's stopping me from preparing a new business plan?

First things first — I would love nothing more than to own a yarn store. But realistically I would need to do a heck of a lot of research and planning before I could open a viable and functional business. I would first and foremost need to have a lot more experience and knowledge of the craft to pass on to my customers. Secondly, I have way too much on my plate at the moment to even contemplate starting another business.

Here's my point: having an idea is one thing, but it doesn't mean you should quit your job tomorrow and rush headlong into organising a business loan. As women, I think we intuitively know within ourselves when the time is right. Sometimes the most successful ventures are those we've dreamt about for years and we've planned them in our minds long before we take the first step. Nothing positive will come of acting with impatience and recklessness when it involves starting a business.

Let's face it — starting a small business is more complicated than any of us could possibly envisage, unless we've lived through the experience with a family member or close friend. Even after this long, I still manage to learn something new every day. One of those very important lessons that I live by is to embrace the fact that I took a chance to do something that inspired me and I really believed in. Unfortunately, it takes more than passion and knowledge to make your idea into a successful business. All successful businesses start with a simple little idea. In order for the idea to flourish, you must stand by it and be determined and confident. Keep in mind that it's never enough just to want to start your own business; it takes a lot more than a good idea and a bit of chutzpah to get things up and running.

Not so unique

Don't be too concerned or put off by the notion that your idea is not original or that there may be something similar in the next suburb or down the street. When I first opened my swim school, I was one of about 10 schools within a 5-kilometre radius. It's more important to make your business concept unique. It should stand out in a crowd of similar concepts. The unique and distinctive difference with my swim school was the location. There were no swimming centres located in major shopping centres within Australia until mine came along (and now there are quite a few). The trick is to do your research and look at enhancing and providing your customers with something a little extra, especially in the initial stages when you are trying to get your business noticed. Take the time to research your idea and look for gaps in the market where you think your idea would squeeze in nicely. As women, I think we know what we would love to have in our cities or suburbs or towns to make our lives a little more pleasant. For example, on a recent trip to Katoomba in the Blue Mountains, NSW, I walked the main street looking for a small convenience store to buy a couple of little goodies for the trip home (you know, a Diet Coke, bag of lollies, etc.). I walked up one side and then down the other, passing countless antique stores, cafés, bookstores, second-hand clothing shops, but no convenience store! Had I passed one and not noticed it, I wondered? Defeated, I concluded that I would just have to stop at a petrol station on the way back to Sydney. Driving in the car, I noticed one of Australia's largest grocery chains located further down the road — we're talking about a 1.5-kilometre walk from the start of the main street to this location (including a gigantic hill). If you were elderly, disabled or didn't have transport, it would be quite an inconvenience to have to travel to a huge store to buy just a few items, especially when it was invariably going to be busy at times. An idea for opening a convenience store is not unique by any stretch of the imagination, but my experience demonstrates that there doesn't appear to be one located in the heart of this beautiful tourist spot. Hopefully, one of you reading this book will venture up that way and take the opportunity to open up a delightful corner store — before I do anyway. This is precisely my point. Your idea doesn't have to be ingenious or inventive. It might be the most obvious and well-used service or product on the market. Your challenge is to find that little niche or point of difference to be successful. Think about what is lacking in your neighbourhood and use this as a basis for your idea.

Asking the tough questions

Before you begin planning and researching, sit down somewhere and really take the time to think about what you are about to undertake. Owning your own business is a life-altering decision for many reasons, so you'll want to make sure you are prepared to start trading with a well-adjusted and focused frame of mind. My best ever swimming races were the ones I had visually and mentally prepared for even before the gun had gone off. This is exactly how your pre-trading mind must be functioning every second of the day. So, find a quiet spot and consider the following questions. Try to answer them with as much honesty as possible.

1. Do you have enough knowledge about your business concept at this moment?

2. Could you research or investigate your concept further? If yes, do you have the time in your current day-to-day responsibilities to do so?

3. Who are your main competitors in your potential market?

4. Are you prepared to learn more about your potential market and if it is viable?

5. Is the timing right to start the business, personally and financially?

6. Will you be comfortable asking for assistance if the need arises?

7. Do you have to make any life-changing decisions that may affect your relationship with someone close to you in order to start your business?

8. Do you have a back-up plan?

9. How will it affect your family?

10. Out of 10, rate how much you want this: 0 — not at all; 5 — kind of; 10 — you dream about it 24/7 and are prepared to do everything necessary to make it come true.

Think about the last question very carefully. If you're not a '10 out of 10' in the preparation and research stage of a new business, then the time may not be right for you to start trading. Your enthusiasm needs to be off the Richter scale for things to gain momentum and have the ability to grow. When I was building the swim school, I would go to bed thinking about it and wake up having dreamt about it. My excitement was palpable and I felt almost crazy with anticipation for the opening day. Have a good think about why you are not at a '10'. What is holding you back? Whatever the reason, that's exactly the area you need to work on before you invest any more time and effort in your dream. You may find that by fixing one particular issue, you will be able to focus without restraint and concern. If you don't attempt to reconcile the issue, be it financial, personal or motivational, then maybe this isn't quite the right time to be making big decisions.

It's far better to address the real emotions that you are dealing with before making a wrong judgement after you've already invested a lot of valuable time and money. This doesn't mean you should stop researching the idea either. Any amount of time spent investigating a possible career change or business idea can only be time well spent, whether you continue down that path or not.

Researching your idea

It would be interesting (and a little sad) to find out how many women have a great entrepreneurial idea or concept that never sees the light of day. Spotting a niche for your idea and having an almost certain guarantee that it will be profitable is an almost impossible scenario for any potential small business owner. This undeniable risk creates instability and uncertainty for any prospective small business and can sometimes make it difficult to get the initial business loan required. This is where your intuition kicks in. You need to be really honest about your business concept. It won't simply be enough to think it might work! You have to be convinced that the knowledge, research and planning that you have carried out has given you the absolute best chance of success. We've all seen small businesses in our local areas that begin strongly but then discontinue after a very short time. Watch these trends because this will be your best gauge of what's happening in the market and in your proposed business location.

What *is* the best way to learn about competitors in your desired marketplace? Short of actually going into their place of business and asking to see their end-of-year financial statements, you can employ less invasive methods to gather important information, not only for research analysis but also for your eventual business plan. I'm no business nerd, but I love to read magazines and articles that keep me up to date with the swimming industry. You don't need to have a registered business or be trading to have subscriptions to magazines or publications in your selected market. You can also simply go online and find thousands of different sites with copious amounts of information dealing with your target industry. By keeping abreast of all the changes and advances in your desired business, you'll never feel like you are playing catch-up with your up-and-running competitors.

Read all about it

If you want to get the low-down on a potential new business venture, here are a few helpful areas to start you on your research path.

- **Trade magazines** You can find these on the internet and at your local newsagency.
- **Trade and business publications** It certainly helps if you are already a member of an organisation. If you are not, you can still search the internet and become a member. Trade organisations will provide you with regular updates and information regarding the market.
- **Subscriptions and newsletters via the internet** It's no secret that I love knitting and that some day I would love to open up a yarn store. I keep myself well educated in 'all things knitting' worldwide by simply subscribing to lots of knitting newsletters.
- **Read a little, learn a lot** If you have seen the movie *Working Girl* starring Melanie Griffiths then you will remember that she was working in a career that didn't really motivate her and her ultimate dream was to move up into the corporate world. One aspect that hit home for me was the fact that she was always reading the newspaper and cutting out articles of interest. Sure enough, one of the articles gave her an amazing idea and (yada, yada, yada) she landed an amazing job and ended up with Harrison Ford as her new boss and new man. OK, it was a movie, but the premise is there. As a result

of watching it, I've become quite the 'scrapbooker' of articles over the past few years — so much so that I had to purchase a filing cabinet for all my good ideas. Many of them are trends within the retail sector that I think may be relevant to me as a business owner. Keep an open mind to any magazines, brochures or newsletters that may come your way or may be idly lying about at a coffee shop — one of them could possibly contain your fabulous new idea or big concept. Most of them will feature fantastic articles about various aspects of business that may assist you in your quest.

Another important factor to consider is how many businesses with your concept are located nearby? If you have done your research and have come to the conclusion that the business nearest to your proposed location looks drab and dilapidated, and therefore success will be yours, you may want to adopt a different mind-set. Take into consideration how long that business has been trading in the area. If they have been there for more than five years, chances are they have built up a loyal and reliable customer base that quite clearly surpasses the business's outward appearance. We have a Thai restaurant located not far from our house that has been there for as long as we have been in the neighbourhood (about 14 years). It's a tad run-down and very tiny, but the food is to die for. About six months ago, a new Thai restaurant opened up 500 metres down the road with all the bright and shiny bells and whistles. Regrettably, it now has a FOR LEASE sign in the window. It's sad when this happens, but it's just a fact of life. Consumers will stick to what they know and love, so make sure you don't have any preconceived ideas about the 'old shop on the corner' that may just be 'the little gold-mine on the corner'.

Research questionnaire

Here are a few questions to ponder before you dive headlong into a new business venture:

1. Do you think you could create a better concept for your customers?

2. What can you offer that others in the same market can't?

3. Are you aiming at the right demographic? Will they love your idea too?

4. Is this neighbourhood saturated with the concept?

5. How popular are your nearest competitors?

6. What marketing have they been doing?

7. Will your prices be competitive with theirs?

Delving and investigating

When I first started to think about opening up my swim school, I remember lying awake at night and wondering if I knew what I was getting myself into. Remember — I had never had a job, so this was fast becoming an extremely daunting task to take on. I knew I had a couple of things going my way — my absolute desire to be my own boss and I knew a lot about swimming. The part that seemed to be an anchor around my leg was the fact that I had no idea how a business operated on a daily basis or where the heck to start. So, I had to do some major investigating — or sticky-beaking may be a more appropriate word for it, I think. I went along to a few different schools in the area and sat for hours and hours watching the general running of the sessions. I didn't have an opportunity (or the nerve) to delve further than purely observing, but this was still a great use of my time in terms of research. I discovered things that seemed to work at the schools and other things that didn't.

Another great way for me to get the initial planning stages underway was to gather as many brochures as possible from swimming schools and associations in the area. Most brochures have mission statements and the all-important 'pricing' on them. This was invaluable because it gave me a solid starting point for my own pricing and helped me improve the mission statement and goals for my school. You should carry out fact-finding expeditions like this to guide you in your financial preparations and to assist with general confidence and organisation. All snippets of information regarding your competitors are going to be like gold, so remember to stay organised and keep all relevant information categorised.

You'll be surprised at what you can find out by doing a little bit of asking around too. If you are not the nosing-around type, there are many ways to gather up information that may be vital in the planning stages for your business. Without question, the internet is probably the fastest and easiest way to start collecting information. Remember: use your imagination! You already have your idea, so go out there and start researching and investigating the ins and outs of your competitors from as many angles as possible. This seems obvious advice, but you'll find that it will be crucial to the whole framework of your business.

Research without leaving home

Thankfully, there are many associations which have already gathered up helpful information to assist budding entrepreneurs. It would really serve you well to investigate the numerous helpful websites on the internet related to developing and planning small businesses. There are sites covering topics that you probably haven't even thought about. While researching this book, I was surprised at the increase in the available information even in the time since I first started planning for my own business. You could almost start a business based purely on the abundance of helpful advice available from various online sites. Here are a few websites worth a look:

- **Australian Bureau of Statistics —
  www.abs.gov.au**: a great starting place, with an abundance of relevant information that you'll most definitely need. You'll revisit this site throughout the time you own your business.
- **Department of Innovation, Industry, Science and Research — www.industry.gov.au**: this website provides wonderful links and detailed reports on similar business types and outcomes in particular demographics. A great way to set the research in motion if you're not the getting-your-hands-dirty type.
- **Flying Solo — www.flyingsolo.com.au**: helpful advice for those just starting out. This site also has a great marketing component to their website.
- **Business.gov.au — www.business.gov.au**: this one is amazing! It's an Australian government initiative and the volume of information will make you feel like you have your own personal advisor. Issues relating to small business can differ from state to state, so this site has wonderful links to information no matter where you live. Remember, things change constantly in small business so keep revisiting to keep up to date with the latest information.
- **Websites for Small Business —
  www.websitesforsmallbusiness.com.au**: a comprehensive website full of great ideas, advice and information, all at very affordable fees. The name says it all!

The internet is without doubt an ideal and super-fast way to gain knowledge about absolutely anything. In terms of researching your direct competitors, it would be more worthwhile and valuable to see and experience things with your own eyes as well as using the internet. Personally, I could have just researched on the internet and learnt everything that I needed to know about all of my competitors without leaving my house. It would have saved me a lot of running around, but there's no way I would have gained anywhere near the same knowledge and insight without observing things with my own eyes. I would have done things entirely the wrong way had I relied purely on my internet research. For example, one swim school had quite a number of children per class to one instructor, whereas another had fewer per class. The level of teaching and the time spent one-on-one per child in a 30-minute class differed quite remarkably. Before observing things firsthand, I would have thought that more children per class equalled more dollars in the register. Instead, I heard quite a few complaints from parents about 'overcrowding' within the lesson. Remember: word travels fast and people talk.

Word of mouth

Never underestimate the importance of 'word of mouth'. It's a major influence on whether a business thrives or withers away. A coffee shop opened down the road from where I live. It was in a convenient spot in terms of location and accessibility, so I decided to stop by after the school drop-off for a takeaway. Unfortunately, I was let down almost immediately. The coffee was ridiculously overpriced and when I took my first sip it was lukewarm and tasted a tad bitter. I was so disappointed because I really wanted this new business to do well. Whenever the topic of great coffee shops came up in conversation, I found myself relaying my bad experience at this particular one.

This is the power of word of mouth — both good and bad. Let your legs do the walking and your eyes do the observing. Research your competitors so you know exactly what you're up against. Don't presume anything in terms of your competitors, especially when you may be hearing it first- or second-hand. One of my greatest bugbears when I first opened my business was the feedback about my operation compared with others. It's important to stay true to yourself and your mission statement, and your customers will form their own, hopefully favourable, opinions.

I never talk badly about my competitors or question why they run their businesses the way they do. It's time-consuming and tiring enough getting your own business exactly the way that you want it, let alone allowing other people's ideas to infiltrate and burden your mind.

My little tips

- Nothing positive will come if you act with impatience and recklessness.
- Find a niche or point of difference with your business idea.
- Visualise and mentally prepare for the challenging road ahead.
- Your enthusiasm and desire should be 10/10. If you have concerns, now is the time to address them.
- Research is your new best friend — don't press the fast-forward button when it comes to investigating and gaining more knowledge about your proposed business venture.
- Don't let the amount of preparation and research required get you down.

Two Failures and
One Success

My first failed business idea

My second failed business idea

My third business idea — success!

Idea questionnaire

My little tips

My first failed business idea

I must have had delusions of grandeur when I had my first great business idea. I was taking a two-week break from swimming after the Atlanta Olympics in 1996 and somehow that time seemed to stretch on longer than I had anticipated. Before I knew it, two weeks had swiftly become two months and my desire to put on a pair of togs and start the whole training regimen once again had completely disappeared from my steadfast and focused mind. I had just moved in with Greg, my fiancé, and he was extremely busy completing his last year of a physiotherapy degree, so I found myself being unusually bored for the first time in my entire life. Greg would come home from uni every day and say, 'So, what did you do today?' I would find myself inventing things that I had done during the day just to appear as though I was completely run off my feet. It was actually embarrassing and depressing to feel like I had nothing to do physically and no goals ahead of me to keep me motivated. For the first time in my life I had no desire to get back into the pool to train, let alone compete ever again. This negative frame of mind is a major crisis for any professional athlete. As well as it being a financial concern, I also had many personal sponsors relying on me to continue competing and excelling. Looking back, I definitely knew that after two months I was making it more difficult to return as every day went by — not only physically, but also mentally. Why would I want to return to cold mornings, freezing winters in the pool, no late nights, no junk food, nothing of anything that was fun? I had finally had a decent taste of a 'normal' life and I wasn't prepared to give it up. I distinctly remember the three-month 'holiday' mark approaching and I went and sat in a park and really thought about what I wanted to do. I had absolutely no qualifications to do anything other than swim, and the sheer reality of looking for a job seemed ridiculous without experience or training. I reluctantly came to the decision that I had no other option but to return to my life as a professional swimmer.

Everyone seemed quite relieved that I had 'come to my senses', but when Monday morning rolled around and my alarm clock started buzzing, I had nothing left in the 'dedication tank'. My mind and body seemed like a dead weight. The feeling of dread was something that I will never forget.

Greg missed his university lectures that day and we sat in our little house. He looked over at me and asked, gingerly, 'Have you thought much about what you'd like to do other than swimming?'

'No,' I solemnly answered, 'I have absolutely no idea what I'm capable of doing or even what I want to do as a career.'

I knew deep down that I was completely exhausted from the life I had led as a swimmer, and to be honest I was not in any way prepared for a life outside of sport. It would be an accurate assessment to say that I was in a complete rut! Competitive swimming had been a sheltered and lonely existence and I now found myself facing a major life dilemma. I did know one thing for certain — I knew that without any doubt I would really struggle holding down a nine-to-five job. I was 22 and the only job that I'd had was at the age of 15 working for six days at a food stand at the Brisbane Show. Over the entire six days, my cheque totalled $143.70, but it may as well have been a million dollars to me. Apart from this, I had absolutely no experience at anything other than following a black line for hours on end. For the first time in my life I felt completely lost. Maybe my only option was to return to swimming, but I wanted to avoid this at all costs. I started thinking about various career paths that might suit my personality and challenge me. I didn't even know what I liked doing because I had done nothing but swim for more than 20 years. My only other interests were baking, reading, exercising and almost anything to do with craft. Maybe I could find myself a job associated with one of these things? Could I work in a bookstore or a bakery all day and be completely satisfied? I knew I couldn't work in a gym or be a personal trainer because that would be too close to the life of a swimmer. I knew I needed to do something that was creative and stimulating — something that would keep me occupied and busy all day long.

My only other option was to create a business involving dogs and dog-walking. I really love dogs, and power-walking had been a main component of my athletic fitness outside the pool. I really started to think about this as a potential business idea. I thought at that moment that I'd just become an entrepreneurial genius. Certainly, there had to be a lot of unhappy pooches sitting at home all day getting no exercise, along with many guilty pooch owners who weren't exercising them. So I started conducting my own market research while walking the streets with my own dogs. Before I knew it, I was down at the local Officeworks printing off flyers, business cards, letterheads and mail-outs without even realising that I might want to do a business plan, apply for an ABN (Australian Business Number), or even have some idea what the heck I was trying to create, especially if I wanted to build this into a properly certified, registered and viable business. I really had absolutely no idea what was involved in owning and operating a legitimate small business.

Needless to say, the business empire of 'Walkin' the Dog' didn't last very long. It didn't *quite* have the customer base (I had a grand total of two dogs to walk), or the enthusiasm for my idea to go anywhere but swiftly down the toilet. The two customers I did have were only charged $5 for a 30-minute walk. I didn't even stop to think that at $5 a pop per dog, I'd need to exercise a lot of pooches before I could even buy myself some lunch, let alone contribute to the mortgage or grow a business. I know these days (compared with the 1990s) dog-walking can be a very profitable venture and looking through the *Yellow Pages*, dog-walkers in the 21st century are asking for a lot more than $5 for their trouble. Like any business, dog-walking obviously requires the correct planning, researching, marketing and perseverance before it can become feasible and successful. Reflecting on that time, not only was I lacking the necessary requirements expected of an entrepreneur, I also had completely no idea what I was doing.

The message here is quite clear and precise: all great ideas need dedication, commitment and planning. You have to put in the time and effort to structure every little aspect of your idea or it just becomes another good idea going nowhere fast. Don't rush out either and spend unnecessary funds on items for the business without first doing a business plan.

NB. If you need some flyers for a dog-walking business, I still have about 2,000 in a cardboard box. What a waste of money that was!

My second failed business idea

I'm actually very embarrassed to tell this story, so I want you to know that I'm including it for educational purposes only. As I clearly demonstrated in the previous story, having a great idea without first engaging in the proper preparation time is a big risk and a definite time-waster. You would imagine having experienced one disastrous business attempt that most people would learn a few significant lessons from such a diabolical mess. In turn, you would think they would avoid making the same mistakes a second time around. Not me!

Back in the brief hiatus between my retirement and starting the swim school I became a sewing maniac. I finally had my head out of chlorine and I had a sudden urge to sew. Could I sew? Well, it depends on your perception of what good sewing entails. I had completed Home Economics in Year 8, where I had made quite a nice little calico bag with my initials sloppily blanket-stitched on the front, but that was about the extent of my sewing prowess. I did, however, own a really expensive sewing machine that I had no idea how to use (principally because I *hate* instruction manuals), which then led to my next big idea — patchwork pillows. The material I bought for them was expensive and utterly gorgeous, but just one of these 'artworks' took me upward of five hours to make. To add a touch of the 'dodgy', I didn't quite know how to put a zip in, so I just added buttons to keep the inner stuffing from bursting out. Martha Stewart would have been mortified to see the end product! I forgot to mention that I didn't even bother overlocking the edges either and the patterns on the pillows were hand-stitched without turning the edges under. Needless to say, there were many 'frayed edges' and the pillows looked like my six-year-old niece had made them. I don't really understand why I thought my pillows were so fantastic and that I was going to be a huge hit at the markets. I would sew until 3 a.m. to make my creations, but I loved every minute of it. Thinking back to this time, I truly believed that any potential customers would find it impossible to walk past my little stall without falling in love with one of my pillows. But as pretty and colourful as they were, my handiwork was pretty shabby, to be perfectly frank. The sad thing was that although I think my husband thought they were quite lame, he didn't have the heart to tell me the truth.

At 3 a.m. on market-day morning, I jumped out of bed excitedly and I drove my car packed full of pillows into the city. I paid $80 rent for a stall and was shown to a handy position under a tree near the river. It took me about an hour to set up and I was so excited in anticipation of all the market-goers eventually arriving and visiting my little table full of patchwork prettiness. I watched a beautiful sunrise and pondered whether my 'pillow empire' was about to become a reality. At 6 a.m. the early marketeers started arriving. My stall looked fantastic, and I had even managed to place the *really* dodgy pillows further to the back so no one would notice — great merchandising! I decided that I was going to sell each pillow for $40. Being mathematically gifted, I worked out that by selling only two pillows I would instantly cover the cost of renting the table space. How could I not be successful with that type of insight? By 9 a.m. my little stall had only managed to intrigue a couple of people, but even those few briskly moved on when they inspected the pillows more closely.

Had they seen the frayed edges and been put off? Embarrassingly, most people would glance and then pretend I wasn't even there. Maybe it could be the location?

My stall was squashed between a handmade jewellery stall and one that sold paintings made from paperbark. Both of these stalls had already made many sales, so I began to think that possibly the patchwork pillows were not a great idea after all. By noon I was bitterly crushed and felt like running away and hiding. Why had I insisted that my entire family come to visit me and see the wonders I'd created? I sat there and pondered my own complete disillusionment. Don't get me wrong — I had experienced failure and embarrassment before, but for some reason this seemed to go beyond anything that had happened previously. My mum is quite an amazing seamstress and even she had managed to convince me that the pillows were pretty and ready for selling. Could my own mum have felt compelled to lie about the fact that my pillows weren't quite the pieces of art I thought they were?

I wanted to make a sale so desperately before my family arrived but time was ticking away. Before I knew it they would arrive and I would have to start lying about the whole debacle. But it was too late! Up marched my husband and son with my parents and parents-in-law in tow. I'm sure I don't even need to paint the picture of humiliation and shame that was stall 97. I really wanted them to arrive and witness a sea of customers queuing at my stall, fighting each other off to grab the last remaining pillows ... But alas, it was not to be! At that moment, I would have gladly welcomed an enormous asteroid to hurtle through the atmosphere and hit the top of my stall, destroying every last pillow. No such luck! I was quickly brought back to reality by Mum's voice.

'How are things going?' she asked, completely shattering my hopes of a heavenly body wiping out the train wreck that was my pillows.

'Yeah, really great, thanks. I've sold four pillows and a lady forgot her purse and is coming back to buy two more of them,' I stated enthusiastically while my pants promptly caught on fire.

'That's quite amazing, dear. I knew you would do well,' she said encouragingly, all the while observing firsthand the sluggishness of trade at my stall. I'm pretty sure I saw a pitiful grimace play across her face while 'an inspection' was taking place, or maybe it was just an expression of sympathy. Either way, I'm sure both my parents were thinking what I had been all morning: *How could a girl go from being lauded by a nation as queen of the pool, to be now selling poorly made pillows at the markets on a Sunday morning?* The embarrassment was engulfing me in a sea of negativity and shame that somehow managed to intensify with each passing second. I met my husband's gaze and no words were necessary as I indicated to him my need for some breathing space.

'Well, you don't need us here bothering you, so we'll come and see you when we leave,' he said with a knowing look.

I was sure he could sense my despair anyway, even without prompting, so the obvious thing for him to do was just to leave me to cope by myself.

'Sure, that's if I haven't sold out of pillows by the time you get back!' I joked, while managing to maintain the best Lady Gaga 'Pokerface' I could muster.

Now I felt even worse. Not only had I lied to my entire family, but no one had approached my stall in the entire 45 minutes they had visited and the bloody 'bark art dude' in the stall beside me was selling things left, right and centre! To pour salt directly into my already gaping wounds, I couldn't even leave to go to the toilet because I was worried someone would steal my pillows (which may have actually been a blessing)!

The day slowly and painfully passed by, when eventually the 'jewellery lady' and the 'bark art dude' started to pack their leftover stock away and began counting their takings. No need for me to do that. I'd started with a float of $150 and had now counted $62 in my little cash tin. Eighty dollars went to the owner of the market for the table and I'd bought two takeaway lattes at $4 each. I had managed to lose $88 and any self-esteem I may have had at the beginning of the day. I did, however, manage to gain a few things throughout that long day — a bladder infection from holding on too long, as well as a painful realisation that beauty really is in the eye of the beholder. The 'beholder' was me, of course — and there were no other beholders anywhere to be found.

What an ordeal! Driving home, I couldn't remember the last time I felt so utterly dimwitted and useless. I didn't even want to go home and face my husband and have to admit to my son that no one loved Mummy's pillows quite as much as he had. I did make it home and hubby was waiting with a lovely dinner and a big cuddle.

'How's my market lady?' he asked.

I didn't need to answer him, as the tears came in buckets and then tidal waves that seemed to cascade down my cheeks like a torrential monsoon. Snorting and sniffling away, I told him about my day and how foolish I now felt. I admitted feeling completely defeated and beaten, and that I couldn't remember the last time I felt so negative and downbeat.

'Why are you so upset?' he consoled. 'So, you didn't have a great day. Stop feeling sorry for yourself and look at the reasons things didn't go well. If you think of starting another venture ever again, make sure you plan it properly next time around. It's not the end of the world, you know.'

I did eventually confess to the rest of my family that I was indeed a flop and apparently they had guessed as much — nothing like a bit of faith! Apart from coming to the realisation that no one liked my pillows except me and my three-year-old son (who didn't realise how poorly they were constructed), I had actually just learnt some valuable lessons in terms of business: Don't take your customers for granted. The stench of 'dodginess' can be smelt a mile away, so don't expect to be an overnight success in an area that isn't quite your forte. In hindsight, I should have at least done a sewing course or been to the markets to see the high-quality items that other vendors were selling. Eleven years on, I still have a couple of the pillows to remind myself of the lessons I learnt that day, and the memories of that particular market are not very far from my family's thoughts when I tell them that I have a new idea for something. 'You're going to sew patchwork pillows and sell them at the markets?' A chorus of fitful laughter ensues at my expense.

'Happy to amuse you all!' I respond.

Lessons were learnt in a big way that day. My new mission, after the dog-walking and the pillow fiasco, was to prepare things properly, and not to be so impatient for 'huge success'. I was hoping that my third attempt at some form of business would be a more positive experience than the first two had been.

My third small business idea — success!

Developing my own swim school was a dream that surfaced way back in 1994 at the age of 20, when I was competing at the Commonwealth Games in Canada. While on a shopping trip to a local mall, I passed a swim school that was located inside one of their major retail centres. I stayed at the facility for hours, mesmerised by the process of children learning to swim, while their parents could leave to enjoy everything the massive centre had on offer, as well as indulge in some retail therapy for themselves — two birds with one stone! This whole concept made perfect business sense. I wondered if this was happening back in my own country, right under my nose! The idea certainly got under my skin and even though at that time in my life I was well and truly entrenched in my swimming career, I was also painfully aware that my body was starting to get tired from the many years of training and competing. I realised that sooner rather than later I had to start thinking of life after swimming.

After my Canadian adventure, I managed to keep relatively free of injury and remained in the sport for a further two years. Before I knew it, another Olympics had rolled around and I spent yet another long block of time with my head submerged in chlorine. Swimming was definitely a full-time job for me, but in hindsight I wish I had completed some part-time courses or at least done some work experience somewhere. When the day finally came to hang up my goggles for good in August 2001, it finally hit me that this time, at age 27, there was definitely no going back to the sport, unlike my previous 'break'. By then, my son was almost four and would be off to kindergarten in the coming months. My husband was working long hours at the local private hospital as a physiotherapist. I certainly loved being a mum, but I felt I needed something to keep my mind active and my body moving. My life had suddenly gone from training and competing, running a household and rarely having an opportunity to sit down, to almost a complete standstill.

About two months into retirement, a good friend of ours who worked in the swimming industry paid us a visit. The conversation turned to swim schools and the need for more in the ever-growing city of Brisbane.

'You should open that swim school you've always talked about,' Greg said, half jokingly.

The room went silent while the three of us sat in the living room waiting for someone to say something. Eyes shifted from one person to the next, and all I could think about were my past failures and how there was absolutely no way I could possibly revisit another 'pillow situation'.

'Well, it would be a very different concept. I can't imagine there would be many pools located in shopping centres in Brisbane — or even the entire country,' I stated.

I realised that the boys weren't going to comment until I did, and unless I really wanted to do it there wouldn't be any need to continue the conversation.

We sat there for hours plotting our strategic plan. Before we knew it, the sun was rising on a new day while also streaming bright light onto our amazing new business idea. Our plan was to approach the leasing managers of one of Australia's largest shopping centre owners — Westfield Group — in the hope of discussing and pitching our concept. Within the week we were meeting with some top executives and proposing an outline of our scheme. We had absolutely no expectations whatsoever, so you can imagine our surprise and joy when a few days after the initial meeting, Westfield agreed to a second, more comprehensive meeting. By this stage, we were quite confident that things were looking positive. As we all sat down, one of the executives turned my way and said:

'We're *very* excited about your idea for a swim school. The company's philosophy is the importance of diversification and growth, and therefore we would like to move forward in finding you a suitable location for the school. After doing that, our vision is for your business to be trading within the next six-month period. What are your thoughts?'

'Um, well … yes!' I replied stupidly, unable to make my mouth form words containing any semblance of intelligence. It would be a monumental understatement if I said that their response was what I had expected.

'I mean to say, that's great news,' I stumbled.

Could I have just bitten off more than I could chew? I hadn't really thought that they would agree to the idea. Only a week had passed since we'd been sitting in our living room brainstorming ideas and now it looked like it was really going to happen.

It was just a little idea that was somehow growing legs and striding forth like Usain Bolt! After that meeting, the whole situation was not dissimilar to a locomotive that had lost its brakes and was careering down the tracks, completely unstoppable. Was this the way normal businesses started? The idea for the pool was unquestionably innovative, but none of us had the knowledge or the experience in small business to know where to start. Needless to say, the next six months travelled by very quickly and before I knew it I had written my first business plan and I actually had a mission statement and plan for the future of the school. Unfortunately, things were not as easy as I had hoped in relation to the building process. Apparently, building a swimming complex inside a shopping centre is not a normal, everyday occurrence so the construction phase was an extremely stressful period. After many sleepless nights, the swim school opened in June 2002, four weeks later than predicted and advertised. (Fortunately, I've managed to bury that episode securely in the confines of my brain.)

After having dramas in the preparation stages of my own business, I now understand why in many circumstances the 'idea phase' is as far as some people ever venture with their own concept. The details and intricacies involved in setting up a business are quite daunting, especially for first-timers. If you are not generally a risk-taker or you don't have a 100-per-cent commitment and belief in yourself and your ability, you may be making a huge mistake by even attempting to start a business. I'm certain that there are many people that live with the fact that an opportunity may have been lost because they didn't follow through with their idea. After the ordeal I went through in those initial preparation months, it was easy to see how budding business owners with great ideas might find it difficult and disconcerting during this stage. For me, not only was it the realisation that we had invested quite a lot of our money to start a business, but the five-year leasing term that we had agreed to also meant that a huge commitment had also been made to another entity. I wouldn't have had the luxury of being able to back out a couple of months down the track, or even a couple of years. This is why it is my mission throughout this book to get you from 'idea phase' to 'operating phase'. Deep down, you probably already know if your idea is a keeper.

The best investment of your time and money is to plan and then plan some more. By then, you should be well and truly confident that your business idea is worth developing.

Idea questionnaire

You've come up with a great idea and now you'd like to know how to progress with it? Ask yourself the following questions to get a clearer picture of what to do next:

1. What is your idea for a small business?

2. Is your idea your current hobby or interest? If so, do you have a back-up hobby to do other than your business idea?

3. Have you told anyone about your idea? If so, what was their reaction and how did that affect you?

4. Why do you think your idea could be successful?

5. Do you think that your idea has a unique or special element to it? If yes, what is it?

6. Do you have any experience in relation to your idea?

7. Could you do more to strengthen your knowledge or experience?

8. Have you researched the competitors in your chosen market environment?

9. Is the market already saturated with similar ideas?

Beware the naysayers! Some people are just born to be 'dream stealers'. When I have an idea, which is quite often, I'm always careful about those I choose to share it with. Throughout life, we unfortunately have certain people that don't want us to succeed for their own reasons. As much as you'd like to reveal your amazing idea to the world, hold off for as long as you can. Only confide in the people that you trust — those that will assist you with the appropriate help and not the kind that will only be a negative distraction. Your idea, as great as it probably is, may or may not be plausible to others, but try not to let this deter you. Take the positive and negative feedback, dissect the parts you think will be useful and discard the rest into the 'advice' bin. If mistakes and bad decisions are to be made, then you can be responsible for making them. The enriching aspect about making those mistakes is that you will invariably learn a great deal from them, and in doing so, you hopefully won't end up replicating them a second time.

Stick firm to your idea and try to maintain a positive frame of mind. Sometimes we have to take a few knocks before we can go all the rounds. After all, how else do we learn and grow and become more aware of what we are capable of achieving in life? Don't be scared to learn. It's imperative that you remember that not everyone can see the complete picture like you can.

My little tips

- Not all your business ideas will be huge successes — don't outlay large amounts of money until you are 100 per cent happy with your preparation.
- Don't be put off by failure — this is how we learn and grow.
- The best investment of your time and money is in planning for everything — avoid any surprises.
- Maintain a positive mind frame.

The Motivation

What is motivation?

I've just returned home from my daily swim at the local pool where I watched an elderly gentleman sit by the pool wearing his old-fashioned trunks with his goggles placed squarely on his wrinkled face. He didn't actually enter the pool for the entire two hours I was there. I watched with great anticipation as he made his way off the bench at least four times and he managed to dip his toe into the pool only then to retreat to his spot on the bench. I carefully observed this scenario before I managed to come to three conclusions:

Number 1: He thought the water was too cold for a swim (impossible in a Brisbane summer with the water still lightly heated, but I would still regard this as a perfectly good reason not to get in);

Number 2: He never intended to swim but to simply soak up the sun by the side of a council pool and only dip his toe in occasionally for fun (unlikely, considering he had managed to come relatively prepared with goggles);

Number 3: He couldn't swim and was trying to find the courage just to get his body wet (very likely).

I finished my swim and was drying myself when the gentleman approached me.

'I've been watching you for hours going up and down and I was sitting there wondering where you could possibly find the motivation to keep going. I swim here most days, but today I arrived with every intention of getting in and swimming my usual kilometre, but I couldn't even get the motivation to get myself wet. I even dipped my toe in and felt how inviting the water was and still couldn't make myself get in!' He was shaking his head as he was talking, and then he looked at me in anticipation that I might have some insight into his predicament.

'I guess it was just one of those days we all have where you just can't find the motivation. Perhaps tomorrow you'll feel differently,' I said to him, almost feeling guilty that I had been driven enough to crank out the laps instead of him.

'Yes, maybe *tomorrow* ...' he replied, less than enthusiastically, before walking away.

By definition, motivation is the activation of goal-orientated behaviour. So, where the heck does it come from? Most of us need it on a daily basis just to complete the mundane tasks we have to perform, like washing, ironing, cleaning, going to work, etc. Some days, you may find that you have an abundance of motivation, plus energy and enthusiasm mixed in for good measure. Other days, it may seem cataclysmic just getting out of bed. This is all pretty normal. It's no great secret that a good night's sleep and eating the right food certainly give us energy, but motivation comes from inside our hearts and our minds. It can't be trained or programmed, but more specifically it must come from within. Any small business owner will tell you that you need bucketfuls of motivation and then some. The levels of motivation and drive are not dissimilar to what is required from a professional athlete. The hours are long, you need to set defined and succinct goals and your success hinges on the amount of effort and dedication that you are willing to put in. There will be days here and there when you wish that you had never had the idea to start your business, but that's when you take the good with the bad and move on. You'll feel a lot better on those less-than-inspiring days if you dig deep into the recesses of your motivation stores and work on.

I'm a big believer in making it a priority to give myself the occasional mini-break here and there if I'm feeling uninspired to go to work. Think of yourself as a car that needs a tune-up every now and again. I think it's perfectly OK to occasionally allow yourself a day to just 'be'. If you have just started out in small business and you don't have the staff to cover you, it will work in your favour to try to get help for just one day. Being motivated is all about rewards and breaks. If you are running on empty and you can't see a light at the end of the tunnel, it's extremely difficult to stay motivated and focused on any tasks.

A person's motivation to succeed or excel at something is usually founded on wanting to improve the quality of their life or the lives of those around them. In order to be successful at this in a business sense, you need to begin with well-defined goals in a whole range of areas. If you're aimlessly travelling along with no idea about the direction you're heading in, how can you possibly have the motivation to keep going when you don't have a destination in sight?

My whole life is based around the levels of motivation needed to reach certain goals or simply 'get things done'. I think I am a driven person in most aspects of my life, mainly because of my years as a swimmer. Reflecting on those years, I would have needed to be on my deathbed if I made the decision not to turn up to training, because that's the only excuse my coach would have accepted. This made it quite easy to find that extra bit of motivation to arrive — the alternative was an unavoidable and nasty confrontation. In hindsight, I should have taken a day off when my body and mind needed to rest, and this is something that I only recognise now as being an important part of the motivation process. You can't physically and mentally keep running on an empty tank. My advice is to do whatever you need to in order to give yourself a rest. You're the only one who can decide whether this must be a complete and utter break, or whether a decadent hot bath and some quality retail therapy will do the trick.

My first tough week

My initial trading week at the swim school was not quite the picture of efficiency and simplicity I had envisioned. I imagined my quaint yet extremely busy business, strategically and conveniently situated within a large shopping centre, would be a place where I'd work for a bit, then go shopping for a bit, and then go back to work for a bit longer. The world would be rosy and the sky would be blue and my life would be filled with cappuccinos and shopping — and maybe a bit of work to fill the gaps in the day! To say I was extremely deluded would have to be the understatement of the year. This is what happens when you live in an 'athlete's bubble' for too long; it's a world devoid of work-related responsibilities. Anything that could go wrong that week, did go wrong. I had staff and customers complaining about anything and everything. I was in a complete state of shock. Not only had I started a business, but I had inadvertently placed myself in a position of authority where decisions and

answers had to be made by the only person accountable —
me. That first week was the longest and most stressful week
of my life. Keep in mind that I'm the mother of two boys
who both had severe reflux as babies and I can tell you that
this, without a hint of a lie, was far worse.

When I reflect on that time, it was a combination of
factors that were completely freaking me out.

Firstly, I'd never had a job in my life, so the 8 a.m.
to 6 p.m. working-behind-a-front-desk part was tiring
mentally.

Secondly, having no experience as an employer was
difficult and I lost count of the number of times in that first
week I had to consult my trusty business books, especially
the chapters called 'Managing Staff'. I struggled to
understand my role and how I was supposed to solve issues
for my employees.

Thirdly, my name was on the business, which meant I
had to be cheery all day long (when most of the time I was
freaking out and exhausted).

Fourthly, I hadn't given myself an exact and precise role
nor had I set a goal to achieve.

Fifthly, not being able to pick up my four-year-old from
pre-school made me feel very guilty.

Lastly, I spent a lot of time wondering if I'd made the
right decision and stressing out that I'd put my little family
under some financial pressure.

I don't want *my* issues to dissuade you in any way from
pressing on with your own dreams. Unless you're a retired
professional athlete or are independently wealthy, you
are already in a better position than I was because you've
probably had a job at some stage. I think the only thing

that kept me motivated was the fact that I knew there was absolutely no option to back out. It also helped that we had friends in small business and they were constantly reminding us that the first months would be all about trying to find our feet and save our sanity. I did have the dedication to realise that I had started something that required persistence; I had common sense and lots of motivation; plus I really was very determined to succeed at something other than competitive swimming. With hindsight, I should have worked at a swim school to gain experience from both an employee and an employer point of view. Don't you just love hindsight?

Anyway, I did things the difficult way and I battled my way through the first testing and forgettable months. I encourage you to acquire any small business advice you can get from friends or family. It would also be an advantage to work in the industry, or an associated one, before you start your business. The confidence gained from this experience will only help with your motivation levels. The more you know and the more comfortable you are can only assist you to have the motivation to improve and excel.

Having the drive and the will to succeed certainly helps to achieve goals, but that alone won't always get you across the line. Bolster yourself with as much small business know-how as possible. Mix drive and knowledge together and you have a killer combination!

When difficult and stressful situations occur — and they probably will — find the will and the desire within to pick yourself up and keep going. This is where setting realistic goals comes in hand. No silver platters here, remember!

Your motivating factor

Stop and think for a moment — what is the motivating factor for wanting to become a small business owner? If you're an impulsive person like I am, then owning a business is a great way to learn patience and perseverance, because it's certainly not a quick and easy ride to happiness or financial freedom. Having said that, many entrepreneurs have gone on to great success because they seized an opportunity, and before they knew it they were running a successful business and living their own dreams, not just wishing for it to happen.

Why does this happen to some people and where can I buy the book that sets me along the same path, one that's devoid of obstacles and distractions? Well, the short answer is you can't ... I've looked! Not only have I searched the shelves of libraries and bookstores nationwide, I have yet to meet a small business owner that has had an easy ride. You'll find that most of the instant business success stories had a lot of luck, were in the right place at the right time and possibly had amazing contacts — basically your one-in-a-million opportunity. Obviously, this situation doesn't come around too often, so it's probably a good idea to assume that if you want to start your own business, you may just have to roll up the old sleeves and plan to get a little dirty.

Ultimately, the decision to start a business rests on your shoulders and therefore the planning and motivation have to come from you. If you are at the point where you are reading this book, then two amazing things are already happening in the universe: firstly, one of *my* major goals has been reached (to have a book published and then someone actually reading it — thank you!); and secondly, you are at the point in your life where you were motivated enough to buy this book and start your own business journey.

I see the 'buying a business book' scenario as similar to joining a gym. You're at that stage where you're motivated, you want to challenge yourself and you've decided to take the next step — well done!

Motivation is a quality that not everyone knows how to use. For some, it's easier to set their sights and goals quite low so they are achievable, and as a result they never get to extend themselves. We are certainly *all* capable of being motivated, but some can utilise this quality with more gusto than others. I'm sure it may have something to do with how much we were encouraged as children, although I have a close girlfriend who received next to no encouragement as a young girl, and now she is a business mogul. Go figure!

Different events and situations that happen over the course of our lives — as children, adolescents and then throughout the teenage years — could also have a significant bearing on our motivation levels. I've met many people that are quite happy with the same nine-to-five job they've always had and they have absolutely no desire to alter anything or to make new goals. I can't work out if I admire them for feeling content about their choice or if I'm dismayed that they don't go out of their minds with boredom. I suppose because I love to be challenged. Maybe I get bored too easily, but I tend to think that a life without challenges and goals is a life half lived. It reminds me of Fran in the Australian movie hit, *Strictly Ballroom*. She's a novice ballroom dancer with dreams of making it to the big time. She finds her way into the arms of the amazing dancer, Scott (played by the charismatic Paul Mercurio), who is vying for a win at the coveted Pan Pacifics. When everyone finds out that Fran is partnering him, not only do they belittle her, they also give her a thousand reasons why she's wasting her time and Scott's big opportunity. Does Fran doubt herself? Of course she does! Who wouldn't under these circumstances, when people are placing doubt and negativity into your mind?

It's only natural to listen to people, but there's a huge difference between 'listening' and 'hearing'. Make sure you choose people very carefully. This choice will make a big impact on your motivation levels when you're starting out, especially in the planning stages. Try to surround yourself with motivated and positive people who encourage you to reach for your dreams and support you when times get tough. If someone close to you is not on the same page, then stop allowing them to deflate your enthusiasm. Their negativity is the fuel that burns your will to succeed. If it becomes unbearable, then find ways to avoid talking about your business goals and ambitions. For some odd reason, there are people who feel uncomfortable and insignificant when they're in the presence of the positive and the driven. They feel the need to knock that enthusiasm down a notch in order to feel better about themselves. My advice is to give such people a wide berth. This is one of my bugbears. I cannot for the life of me understand why people need to pull other people down in order to puff themselves up. I think it's completely selfish and vindictive. Avoid these people at all costs — they are motivation-zappers!

Motivation training program

This isn't an opportunity for me to include some health advice into my book, but let's be honest: you need strength on the days when things seem hopeless and your dream starts losing its lustre. We all know (because it gets drummed into our brains each day through print media and television) that healthy eating and adequate exercise is the best way to achieve a long and productive life. By following this good advice, not only do we set a positive example for our children but we also add years to our lives. There's nothing worse than waking up on a Monday morning feeling sluggish and tired. Fatigue is a small business owner's worst enemy. Let me just have my moment to be the Commando of thy Entrepreneur!

ALERT! Blatant health advice to follow

If you consume 1,200 calories per day and burn off 1,200 calories per day then you maintain your weight. If you consume 1,200 calories per day and burn off 200 calories per day then your body puts on weight. It really is a no-brainer! You've probably heard it time and time again — energy in, energy out. There really is no deep, dark secret associated with maintaining a healthy weight. I really don't wish to preach the 'health and well-being' issue, but I'm only bringing it up because of the obvious demands that running a business puts on your mind and body. My recent hosting role on a weight loss show has quite clearly shown me the effects poor health can have on energy levels. I'm telling you now, owning a small business makes you both mentally and physically tired. Your mind needs to be sharp and ready for action and there's no better way to be sharper than to have a healthy body. Nothing fatigues the mind and body more than eating bad food and getting too little sleep.

Not long ago, I was having one of those days at work when one frustrating thing would happen every 15 minutes. I had a killer of a stress headache, there was a steady stream of needy customers at the front desk and two of my staff were having a minor domestic in the back room that I'd been adjudicating every spare second. To make matters worse, the clock struck midday and I hadn't eaten breakfast or had any water to hydrate my body. You need to look after yourself for the success of your business. If you are tired and lethargic, your employees and your customers will ultimately pay for it. It's vital to your business that you project a happy, confident and upbeat personality at all times. I'm really sorry to preach this, but it's all true.

Friends of mine own a newsagency and they are pretty much workaholics. One rises at 3 a.m. to do the paper run and the other starts at 5 a.m. to open the shop. They both drag their weary bodies into bed at 11 o'clock at night and suffer from a lack of exercise, too much stress and complete exhaustion — and they're only in their mid-30s! Please factor in a health regime before you start your business. You can be the most successful mogul or multi-millionairess in the world, but if you don't have your health, then the success, money, mansions and Ferraris won't mean a thing — especially if you have a family. You also owe it to yourself to be the very best you can be, and generally that means a 'healthy you', the you that will be around for a long, long time.

Take the time to reassess your goals and think about what is motivating you to start out on your own. Examine your intentions and remember that this is not the time to take risks. It may be a good idea to really think about what you hope to achieve out of your business. Remember to factor in the sometimes unexpected events that may stand in the way of you achieving some of the major goals. I remember one of my goals before starting the swim school was to have another business plan written for an alternative business. I didn't factor in that I would fall pregnant only five months after the business opened — goodbye alternative plan! When I gave birth to my second child, I very quickly realised how much I had changed in terms of what I needed in my life. I wanted my family and certainly didn't want more stress or time away from my family, so I re-evaluated my goals entirely. I didn't foresee *The Biggest Loser* happening, but even before that role was considered, I hadn't factored in any business expansion.

I guess it's kind of crazy not wanting to grow my business, but I am content with my little swim school and not prepared to put my name on another school and have someone else run it somewhat like a franchise. I may be a poor example of a business mogul, but I think it's really difficult to maintain quality in an area as important as teaching children to swim. I think when all is said and done, I'm a person who feels satisfied just to 'be'. If when travelling along I encounter only a few bumps here or there, why start adding some massive road blocks and speed humps to the ride! You may want to assess where you sit in terms of future expansion.

Motivation questionnaire

Is your motivation up to the task? Honestly ask yourself the following questions and consider how important it is to have sufficient get-up-and-go.

1. How long have you been motivated to start your own business?

2. What is the main motivation in starting your own business (e.g. financial security, flexibility, fulfilling a dream)?

3. What is your ultimate goal for starting a business? Do you have a great support team around you?

4. Are you motivated enough to ignore any negativity?

5. Why did you lose motivation in your previous job?

6. What was the last thing/event you were motivated to finish? What was the outcome?

Have a little think about the way you answered this last question because it may be significant to your level of motivation. I recently read a magazine dedicated to running that had a story about a young lady who weighed 99.8 kilograms. She had struggled to lose weight the majority of her adult life and had started many diets but never had the motivation to keep going beyond a few days. One day, she was sent a running magazine in the mail in place of her usual cooking magazine subscription. She rang the distributors, who in turn promised they would send the cooking magazine that day and that she should keep the running magazine she'd received in error. She giggled at the irony of the mix-up but decided to read the magazine even though she had never owned a pair of running shoes. She didn't find anything of interest until the very last pages, where there was a list of fun runs in her area. For some reason, a switch flicked inside her and she felt motivated almost instantly to go and purchase a pair of shoes and begin walking the next day in preparation. She confided in no one about her intentions. Within a few months of training and eating properly she had managed to lose 20 kilograms and completed the 5-kilometre fun run. So, what triggered the motivation? Even she didn't know. And that is the way motivation works. You can have a heightened sense of motivation one day and be as flat as tack the next. That's OK — don't freak out! It's just your mind telling you that you need to have a break from life in general. Motivation is not like a light that can be switched on and off. Your mind needs to be 100 per cent ready and committed to attempt a set goal or task.

Get to it!

I love notebooks, idea pads and all things stationery. I usually can't wait to purchase a new crisp notebook to kick off a new plan or to help motivate me on a new project. I would recommend purchasing a whiteboard. Put it up in your office or study to keep track of all the things that are motivating you to implement new ideas or strategies within your business. Seeing things written down and planned out makes them seem less complicated. If you're anything like me, I often have these wonderful and innovative ideas but can never quite remember them unless I write them down.

Again, the internet is a great resource. There are tons of fantastic websites and software programs available to help get you organised. A great one is www.organisedhome.com, which has amazing forms to print out, calendars, to-do lists and heaps more.

Here's an example of a very simple Excel spreadsheet that you can keep in your diary or print out to post on your wall:

Week starting 25/2	Jobs to get done	Completion date
Monday	Meet with designer	2 March
Tuesday	Order new stock	3 March
Wednesday	Pick up samples	5 March
Thursday	Organise new roster	7 March
Friday	Easter merchandising	In front display by 15/3
Saturday	Prepare for new staff to begin	18 March
Sunday	Go to printers	22 March

The right choices

As I've mentioned before, different things motivate us for a variety of reasons. In terms of the magnitude, you need to make sure that the real rationale behind your desire to start a small business is the right one and that you are doing it for the right reasons. I've definitely been impulsive in the past and I've made some spontaneous decisions. Generally, the wrong choices have been made without a great deal of thought. Make sure you speak to a lot of people within the small business community before you make any quick decisions in terms of your future. Your strength will be tested on a daily basis, in so many different ways. It's no wonder we all seek a change of pace or outlook in our day-to-day lives. It takes a lot of motivation to get through these down times, but certainly starting a new venture will ignite your passions again. Try to make sound choices for the right reasons and not hasty, ill-considered ones.

Financial motivation

Let me say at the outset that starting a new business or buying an existing business or franchise in the hope it will rescue you from financial mess is definitely not the greatest move in the world. It can be very risky and dangerous, and it's probably a good idea to get some financial advice before you press on. I won't pretend to be a financial guru, but I have known a few failed business owners who have fallen into this trap. In my own experience, I certainly know how grateful I was in those initial years that my husband was bringing in a solid and steady income from his physiotherapy practice. I wasn't losing money from the swim school, but I wasn't making a substantial amount that my family could survive on alone.

Things may go your way right from the start and financial bliss may come knocking on your storefront immediately. I would love this to happen for you! You just need to be cautious, do your homework and set in place right from the beginning your financial requirements and goals.

It goes without saying that every budding entrepreneur in the world wants to make money when they start out in business. There's a difference, however, between *making* money from your small business and *surviving*. Merely hoping that you're going to earn some money in order to make ends meet is not a great beginning. There's absolutely no joy or peace of mind in just scraping through at the end of the week. You want to be able to start your new venture knowing that if something unexpected pops up, you have a nice reserve of cash.

When I was preparing my business plan for the swim school, I did a projected monthly budget for the business. Some things were quite easy to calculate because the costs didn't vary each month — for example rent, insurance, etc. With other things, I pretty much had to guess my way through and then adjust by the month when the actual costs starting coming in. Always remember to have some cash in reserve for those unanticipated events that pop up. You don't want your business flailing because one unforeseen incident cost the business money you hadn't expected. After six months of trading, my pool heater broke down and the problem was not fully covered by warranty (that's another story!) and I had to fork out over $2,500 in repair costs. This was one of those unexpected costs that I hadn't factored into the budget.

Take time to consider your current living costs and situation. Think about things logically. If you're barely making ends meet at the moment, or if your credit cards are maxed out and you owe other financial institutions money, then financing a new business or buying into an existing one could be a major risk for you. You'd have to be pretty confident that your business did well from day one and that no out-of-the-blue costs drained your reserve. Factor in your personal living budget as well when you're preparing a budget for your new business. If you are going to be stretched in both areas, consider holding off on the business until you have strength in your bank account. Trust me — you'll be very glad that you waited.

'I'm sick of my boss' motivation

I don't have a lot of personal career advice in this area, but I certainly have friends that started their own businesses because they hated their bosses and thought that they could do a better job. Starting a new business should never be considered purely on a whim or because you might be disheartened by your current workplace or employer. This shouldn't be your sole reason to start a business and it certainly shouldn't be the way to prove a point or 'show them' that you can be successful on your own. There were days during my swimming career that I absolutely despised my coach and honestly thought I could do a better job on my own. Of course, this was ludicrous, and within a few days things were back to normal.

If you're unhappy in your current workplace or dissatisfied with the supervision or direction you're receiving from your boss or supervisor, then try to remove yourself if it's at all possible. Obviously, you need to think things through before you jump the gun. From a boss's perspective, I recently had an amazing swimming instructor leave after six years at the swim school. We didn't have a falling out, but I knew his eventual goal was to move on to a bigger pool facility, which was fine. I was shocked when he eventually handed in his resignation and I was completely knocked for six when I heard he was contemplating starting his own business. Don't get me wrong, he was an amazing employee, but I knew deep down that he didn't quite realise what was involved in the day-to-day running of a business, let alone all the hidden costs involved. Needless to say, he didn't prepare a proper business plan or have any real idea in terms of a budget, so his dream of a small business was abruptly forgotten. Keep in mind that if things seem annoying and stressful from an employee's perspective, then things may not be as rosy from your boss's viewpoint either. The grass is not always greener on the other side. Maybe it's not your boss that has the issues — it could be you!

Case study: Kylie Johnson

Kylie Johnson is a young entrepreneur with loads of motivation. She truly epitomises a strength of character and an enduring commitment and dedication to her craft that now sees her reaping the personal rewards she set out to achieve. As many designers and artists know all too well, it can take years of concentrated time and energy to develop and grow a product or brand. Even then, there

are no guarantees that success will be waiting with open arms. Many talented artisans never get to see their dreams go the distance and therefore never attain the greatness they probably deserve. This is why there is much to be admired about those who reach prominence in their chosen field. It's probably also important to add that many who enjoy success have not had it laid at their feet. Their commitment and dedication, at times when others would have conceded defeat, is remarkable and commendable.

Kylie is one such lady. I'd purchased her gorgeous homemade pottery, inscribed with her serene and thoughtful poems and quotes, but never would have imagined that I'd have the opportunity to meet the accomplished designer in the flesh.

I met Kylie at her home-cum-studio and instantly got the impression that she's more than comfortable receiving guests into her space. She exuded warmth and friendliness and I knew instantly that I'd just met someone extraordinary. I couldn't help but feel in awe of her accomplishments, as well as inspired by her motivational work ethic. I wasn't at all surprised that such a beautiful, whimsical and thoughtful brand such as Paper Boat Press came from such a lovely person.

KYLIE JOHNSON

PAPER BOAT PRESS

Have you always been inspired to design and be creative, and if so, how did you get started? When did you know that you had a talent and flair for design?

My grandma often says that I was born with a pencil in my hand, and even before I had memories of drawing and writing my family all had stories of a 'creativity' that would flow from me. I remember that I went to a writer's camp when I was in Grade Six and in order to be accepted, you had to submit a sample of your writing. I submitted three of my original poems — all of which I *still* know off by heart — and they accepted me immediately. All of this, combined with the unwavering support from both a creative mother and journalist father, my creativity flourished.

Has the idea for Paper Boat Press or your own business always been your dream?

I suppose I have always known I wanted to do something creative. When I was leaving high school I hoped I would be an art teacher, filmmaker, or an artist. I ended up doing Visual Arts at university where I majored in painting and minored in film. I also completed a post-graduate degree in film and television production (I wrote a few seasons for a children's television show, and now am very much a film buff), but art was always where my heart was.

Coincidentally, I met a friend at art college who came from a family of potters. It was here that my love of ceramics was rekindled and the simple fact that both my parents had been potters themselves meant my love and passion for the craft felt very natural for me. I was also a part of a collective group of friends and artists throughout the 90s and early 2000s known as Amfora. We held many group shows and I found this to be a wonderful support network of artists, painters, dreamers and friends. After the group disbanded, I still felt completely motivated to create and pursue my passion for ceramics. Throughout the years, I learnt many artistic skills and had the opportunity to create pottery in the studio as well. It was during this time that I started to envision my own range of ceramics. By this point, clay had metaphorically claimed me and had quite literally got under my nails. I wasn't prepared to let it go for anything.

How important is it to have the support of family and friends?

In one word ... incredibly! My parents have never once questioned (even when I was leaving school) that a creative path wasn't worthwhile. For their love and guidance, I will forever feel very blessed. Throughout my business and adult life, my friends and family have been nothing but proud and supportive, which invariably gives me the courage to keep working and believing that what I am doing is worthwhile and making a difference. These days I have about eight friends working in and out of my studio (as paid contractors) and they are all completely supportive, hardworking and great company. I love every minute working with them and Paper Boat Press would not be what it is without them.

Is it difficult or easy to create and manufacture your own products?

It has been difficult and easy — both, really. It's easy because it's my passion and in my heart, but it's hard work. It's especially hard to create something that is unique these days, especially with the internet and the amount of beautiful work out there. I have to stand out from the crowd, make a statement in the marketplace and also make a living from it. You have to do a lot of things to keep it in motion.

It's taken me a long time to make a living from my work. I have worked part-time as a shop assistant most of my adult life, only in the past two years taking the big step to let it be a full-time occupation. This has been mostly from a financial point of view; I knew if my bills and rent were paid it would take the financial stress off the creative part of my life. It was also a great learning curve because being in retail I learnt many things — pricing, what people want to pay, what they won't pay for, why they buy things, motivation, etc. As a shop girl you also learn how to display merchandise and how point of sale is an important component of a manufactured range. You learn how shopkeepers put your work out for sale, if they display it in a particular way, etc.

Keeping the manufacturing going as your business grows is important. I had to realise that there was only so much I could make with my own hands. I had to get different people onboard to help with the many steps in the process. I had to purchase more equipment, make sure I had back-up equipment and stock if needed. Most of all, I had to not be afraid of the business growing.

What inspired the Paper Boat Press range?
I think it often comes back to my love of words, and inspiring ones at that. I have always wanted to create something that is beautifully made, well made, locally made, made with love and also something that is most of the time affordable to most people. A small piece of art and inspiration for $12.95 ...

Do you have any advice for women hoping to break through with their own designs?

I think the main thing, especially with an artistic career, is that you have to find a way of creating a style of your own ... a brand, really ... even if you are using a medium that a lot of people use. For me, it's clay, paper and words. Find a colour range, a style, a look that is yours, even if other people are doing similar things. Create work that isn't with a base of designs and pattern that can be sourced anywhere. I'm lucky that my 'quote tag' range, for example, has a look and style of its own, and although there has been similar stuff around the place, my work has been in the marketplace long enough now that it has its own life and place. I know my stockists around the country like my work for a number of reasons, most often because it sells well for them. But it's also a point of difference among the other stock that's around.

What is the most important thing you have learnt?

The other day when I was preparing a talk for a women's business function, I thought the thing I wanted to tell them is to work with current technology as though you don't have it. I started Paper Boat Press before the internet as we know it now. Not everyone had a computer (I didn't). There were fax machines, but I didn't own one of those either. I had to make contact and form good relationships with my stockists via telephone and the product info sent through the mail.

So much has changed in the way we communicate — the networking, the instant spread of information, publicity. But you need to remember that it's the goodness and kindness you express, that 'going the extra mile' ... that's what makes a difference. It's the lasting and ongoing sales.

This relies on good product design and manufacture, but it's also the point of sale, whether online, via stockists, or markets, where the relationships that I have formed and the loyalty I have with my stores and customers is still the most rewarding and strong thing.

Was it difficult to stay motivated, particularly when you were starting out?

In a word — YES! Even now, with my career at this point, it's hard. At present I work from my home, but I make sure when I go into the studio I am dressed and prepared for work. There are times when I mooch around in my PJs, but more often to keep motivated I work as if I am leaving the house to work. My team of studio helpers keeps me motivated — that's a real bonus now that my work has grown. Making sure the rent is paid is a big motivator, but I've never done the work to be rich, and I'm still a long way (if ever) from that. I try to keep remembering that I worked hard to get to this point.

How important is a good website and blog?

In this day and age, having a website is very important — the blog, not so much, but that's just my opinion. I use my blog as a journal, a point of inspiration and for news. There are so many blogs, so if you have one, my advice is to keep it simple, inspiring, related to your work, and informative.

Do you constantly set goals for yourself and Paper Boat Press?

I find myself setting new goals and dreams daily! I think I try to keep my goals realistic. I aim high, but know that hard work, will, kindness and spirit always keep me in good stead. My goal was always to make a living from my work, and I'm there now. It only took 20 years! All good things take time. Some steps are getting easier now as my skills, profile and business have hit their stride, but I am always realistic that you never know what's around the corner. And it's a blessing that I'm making a living from what I love — a blessing and a gift that I treasure and respect every day.

My little tips

- Motivation comes from the heart, so make it your priority to use it and not waste time.
- Allow yourself the opportunity to refresh and recharge by planning a break, a mini-holiday or relaxation time.
- You need to have well-defined goals in order to feel motivated and challenged.
- Set realistic goals.
- Avoid people that zap your motivation.
- Look after yourself. A healthy body and mind will serve you well as a business owner — don't take sleeping and eating well for granted.
- Be organised — a cluttered environment won't assist motivation.

Timing

What is timing all about?

My 'timing' moment

Timing questionnaire

My little tips

What is timing all about?

Getting the timing right is extremely important to the success of a new business. As with most things in our lives — relationships, jobs, marriage, babies, career — the correct timing is crucial for giving things the best chance of being harmonious and successful. Make sure you have thought thoroughly about your whole business concept and whether the time is right to start your venture. As women, we have 'extra' little things that we need to deal with as well as juggling a business. The timing of my second baby was very badly planned (well, it wasn't planned would be closer to the truth). I opened the school in June 2002 and found out that I was pregnant with my second child in December of that same year. Most small business owners say that those initial months and years are without doubt the 'teething years', so you need to consider your personal life very carefully and where you sit within the whole 'family' concept. If life is a juggling act for you now and you don't have children, you need to consider at what point during the course of your business you will decide to start trying for a family. When I found out I was pregnant, I thought things would be sweet and everything would fall into place by the time my son arrived. Well, that nine months went by in the blink of an eye and I found myself still reorganising rosters at 39 weeks' pregnant. There are other considerations too, including the intentions of your staff and whether they are going to abandon you at a crucial time during your pregnancy or in a crisis. Your pregnancy may come with its own challenges as well, including medical complications or having to cope with a premature delivery. I'm not trying to instil fear, but rather making sure you are prepared for anything to happen — good or bad.

Being responsible for a business is time-consuming and at times quite stressful, which is why it is important to consider where you sit on the whole 'personal life' front. You need to assess the personality of your partner/husband/boyfriend and how they are going to cope with the possibility of seeing less of you, as well as the likelihood that you'll be a little preoccupied and tired at times. Chances are you may be so organised and well prepared (hopefully because I have geared you up for the worst to happen) that you won't feel any stress or pressure whatsoever. I'm just planting tiny seeds in your mind to be prepared for the negative feelings you may encounter from your significant other if you never seem to be around in the early days. If you are in a solid and caring relationship, then of course the attention that you show your new venture will be necessary and justified. If this isn't the case, you need to be sure that you aren't neglecting the people around you. They will be the ones you'll turn to when you need a shoulder to cry on. After all, I imagine the reasons behind wanting your own business is to: a) bring you happiness; and b) set up you and your family (or soon-to-be family) for a great financial future. If you're already getting that niggling feeling that your significant other may be getting annoyed at you for taking this challenge, then I would strongly advise that you sit down and discuss the situation from both sides. You don't want to find yourself deeply entrenched in starting up your own business, only for them to start getting 'funny' about the whole thing. The strength of your business depends on the patience and support of those closest to you.

My 'timing' moment

When you think about it, most things that we do in our daily lives are all about 'timing'. We schedule and program our lives around so many things these days and getting it to flow nicely can be quite a juggling act. The same can be said about starting a new business or project. We tend to start a new job because the timing is right to leave the old one. We get engaged or married and start families because the time is right in our lives to do so.

I remember being at the shops with my husband, Greg, and my youngest son, Kai, hoping to get a phone call to let me know if I'd secured the hosting role on *The Biggest Loser*. When the mobile rang, we literally all jumped at the same moment. I didn't want to answer the phone for two reasons. Firstly, if I didn't get the job I knew that I would be really disappointed at a missed opportunity. Secondly, I wasn't convinced that the timing was right — I was being offered a job that involved living in another state, away from my family, for the best part of six months. Had I really had a chance to think about whether the job was what I needed and wanted in my life at this moment?

Needless to say, I did get the job, so we ventured over to the food area (where I felt obliged to eat something healthy) and the three of us sat there not knowing what to say. I was not prepared to tell Kai that I would be going away (timing); I didn't want to discuss being apart from Greg (timing); and I didn't want to talk about the job (time away). So, it was all about getting the timing right for everything. Thankfully, my husband squeezed my hand and told me that we would talk about everything once more information came to hand.

Everything in life, especially big changes like starting a new job or planning for a new business, needs to be timed to perfection. I know that I couldn't live without my watch and diary. I'm quite sure that every busy female is in the same boat. Our lives run by the clock, whether it be with our family, our work or our social lives. I believe you'll know instinctively when the timing is right for your new business. If you are still having reservations or doubts, you may need to consider that the timing is not quite right. Take the time to reflect on all areas of your life — personal, children, family, social and other commitments — and think about whether running a new business can fit into your current life and schedule. The pieces of the puzzle need to fit together nicely before you proceed.

The timing of trends

If you read (and believe) current media reports, starting up a new business inside a shopping centre complex at this time could be a high-risk venture. Most situations need to be considered on their own merits and you need to look at outside influences that may challenge the timing of your business start-up. For me, the swim-school opportunity was almost a lucky twist of fate — something I couldn't let pass without serious consideration. The retail sector was booming in 2002 and Australians were spending more time at shopping centres than ever before. I won't lie and pretend that this wasn't a major factor in our decision. Sure, my husband and I could have purchased a block of land in suburbia and built our swim school there, but the obvious increase in shopping activity and the extension of trading hours (major stores had just started opening on Sundays) were important influences on why we chose to start the business at a busy shopping precinct.

Personal timing is crucial but so are the market trends that influence your business. If the timing doesn't suit everything that's going on in your world, don't move forward until you are absolutely sure it's the right fit.

Timing questionnaire

Timing is vitally important. Before you make your decision, consider the following questions:

1. Reviewing your current personal and social life, is it a positive time to start your own business?

2. Are there other issues in your life that may pose problems in terms of the amount of time you will need to dedicate to your new venture?

3. This is a big step. Is it the time right, in your opinion?

4. Would you be in a better position to start a business if you waited six to 12 months?

5. Do you feel all your stars are aligning at this point in your life? Can you dedicate your energy towards a small business?

6. Do you have important goals that you're still keen to achieve? Might they take focus off the preparation of your business? If so, are you able to juggle both commitments?

My little tips

- Let your instincts guide you in terms of the right timing for starting your new venture.
- If you have any reservations, do not proceed until the timing feels right.
- If the timing doesn't feel right, it may be that you don't have all the information you need to proceed at this time. Re-read the research section in Chapter 2.
- Life is unpredictable, but you can create your own destiny with a well-thought-out and orchestrated timeline.

6

Setting Goals and Treating Yourself

What is a goal and what is treating yourself?

Even if you weren't an athlete in your younger years, chances are you had a goal or two out there somewhere. Whether it was related to school, work, money or even family, we all have set ourselves small or sometimes large benchmarks to achieve along our life journey. Goal-setting is a major component of many people's lives, and in some cases it can mean the difference between coping and not coping.

In workplaces across Australia, budgets or targets must be met each month if a business is to function effectively and enjoy prosperity. The employees need to achieve specific goals, day to day, week to week, in order to make this happen. The complete process of goal-setting is a major part of our social and personal development. On a personal and working level, setting goals allows people to identify their own objectives and then decide how diligent they are going to be in achieving them. The true test of being able to achieve those goals depends purely on the level of effort and perseverance a person can find within themselves.

Some of you may be thinking that you're not a goal-orientated person and that setting goals is simply not necessary. I challenge any woman reading this now to admit that they haven't, at some stage in their life, made a personal goal to achieve, be it to eat more healthily, exercise more regularly, spend more time with family, travel, or simply have some 'me' time. So, how do you set a goal and how high should you aim? Most of us set our goals either way too low or way too high, and this does us absolutely no favours. Effective goal-setting is really quite simple —

aim for just a little bit above what you hope to achieve; somewhere around the middle but just a bit above. Start with an achievable goal and then once that is reached, aim higher and challenge yourself more as you attain each benchmark. You will only put yourself at risk by aiming too high. Sometimes this can lead to disappointment and the all-important goal-setting process is avoided in the future.

When I started my weight-loss challenge after my first baby was born, I wasn't unrealistic by setting myself an impossible goal that I could never achieve. In the beginning I aimed for half a kilo each week over 20 weeks as a goal — healthy, realistic and attainable; not impossible, drastic and stressful! I think it's also very important to give yourself little rewards along the way. I allowed myself a new outfit after every 5 kilograms I lost and that was enough to spur me on until the ultimate goal was achieved — four new outfits gained and a healthier, 20-kilo lighter me!

I'm also rewarding myself as you read this paragraph. You see, this is my first book and because I was always out of the country swimming when school assignments were due, I've never had any experience in writing anything more than about 1,000 words (my initial business plan). When I started writing this book, I decided I'd give myself little treats whenever I reached a milestone in the 'word count' department. Tap, tap, tap. I've now reached 30,000 words — well done, Hayley! This means a trip into the city tomorrow for a new Filofax diary. Fun, isn't it? We all deserve to treat ourselves for whatever reason every so often, and in any way that makes us feel good. We all love feeling positive and

unfortunately not everyone around you is going to be aware that you have achieved a 'mini' goal. This gives you a perfect excuse to give yourself a pat on the back and go out and reward yourself.

Not everyone feels the need to treat themselves, but the best thing about reaching a goal, no matter how big or small, is the pride you feel after achieving the result. It certainly provides a natural 'high' that makes your body crave more. Achieving one goal at a time can also start a 'snowball effect' of success. You'll soon realise how important goal-setting is in small business. In the first six months of running my swim school I certainly didn't have any fixed goals for where I wanted to be in one year, five years or beyond. BIG MISTAKE! I now realise that I should have been making goals before I opened the front doors.

With nine years' experience now under my belt, I wouldn't consider starting another business without setting clear and precise goals. I *should* have realised the power of setting goals in business because I knew my best results in the pool were achieved through hard work, goal-setting and visualisation. The best piece of advice I can give you in relation to setting goals is to keep them to yourself. I remember a journalist asking me about my goals going into a particular swimming meet. I blurted out my hopes and expectations and before I knew it there was an article in the newspaper outlining all my innermost thoughts. Big mistake! Without realising it, I'd put myself under unnecessary pressure. It was a lesson well learnt and I stayed quiet after that.

Only share your goals with people that you know will be positive and supportive. Nothing is worse than feeling as though you've lost control of your goals and then having the added burden of others knowing you may not have reached them. Remember to keep goals realistic as well. It's easy to get carried away when you're excited and positive, but then when issues pop up and the excitement turns to concern and disappointment, the small and realistic goals will still seem unreachable. An important part of working towards a goal is to surround yourself with people who will be a positive influence in your life. Imagine yourself surrounded only by people that bolster you and keep your spirits running high and your attitude positive! These are the ones that you need to have close to your side. Try to maintain a space between you and the negative and pessimistic people who may not want success to come your way.

A goal I should have kept secret

When I was in my mid-30s, with my eldest son barrelling towards teenage years, I started to have a mini mid-life crisis. Actually, I don't really know if it was a crisis, more like a 'moment'. (A crisis was when I found a grey hair on the crown of my head at age 26.) Anyway, my son Jacob and I were watching *A Current Affair* and Elle McPherson was being interviewed. In the interview she mentioned her sons aged seven and 12 and Jacob commented that I also had two sons exactly the same age.

'God, she must have had her eldest son at a really young age!' he added.

'Why, do you think she is younger than me?' I asked, thinking there was no possible way that he was going to say 'yes', considering Elle is ten years *older* than me.

'I guess she looks about five years younger than you,' he stated quite convincingly.

Come on! I know she's gorgeous, but did my son really look at me and think I looked older than a woman in her mid-40s? I promptly excused myself and ran to the bathroom and inspected my sun-damaged face (thanks to hours of swimming training in the sun) as well as my dimply legs and thighs (thanks doughnuts and chocolates). I really felt terrible!

Right, what was I going to do to rectify this situation? The next morning I bought myself a wide-brimmed hat and some high-protection zinc cream (with Elle on the packaging as a reminder) and set a goal to lose the dimples (cellulite is the more precise term). I'd never been a runner but had read in most health journals than running and skipping were the best ways to lose weight around the thigh region. I wasn't completely delusional about my ultimate objective either. I knew that I was never going to look like a supermodel but my son's innocent comment had given me a swift kick up the backside! I set myself a goal (not weight-related but more clothing-related). I really wanted to fit into a pair of jeans that I had purchased on eBay that I couldn't even get to fit over my calves. I've found clothing goals are much less stressful than weight-related goals. Before I knew it, I was actually enjoying my daily runs and more of my clothes were now requiring a belt — an accessory that I'd never before required thanks to my thighs acting as a shelf to keep my jeans up.

I'd never been into 'land based' fitness, so to say that I was ecstatic not to smell of chlorine after doing exercise was an understatement. Being a goal-orientated person, however, I now made the crucial mistake of telling people that I wanted to run a half marathon. Why did I feel the need to tell people my personal goals? Needless to say, the questions and comments soon followed:

'I heard you were running a marathon!' or 'When is your big race?' 'What time do you think you will do?' and even, 'Do you think you'll make it?'

Talk about the Spanish inquisition! This had become a nightmare. Now I *had* to run it and a small personal goal had quickly become everyone's business. I'm approaching 40 and I still continue to learn! So, as far as telling people your plans, the best and most honest advice I can pass on is to keep your goals on the 'down low'. If you're someone that thrives on attention and pressure, then by all means take out an advertisement in the *Sydney Morning Herald* and announce your intentions to the country. If you're anything like me, then advertise your goals on a piece of paper and hide it away in a place that only you will look. I must admit, I tell my husband most things but I have learnt since the Pillow-gate event (see Chapter 2) to keep any major goals or plans to myself until success is almost knocking on my door.

When it doesn't happen overnight

Just like Rachel Hunter in the Pantene shampoo commercial years ago, it won't happen overnight, but it will happen — hopefully. I really don't want to be the bubble-burster here, but success may not happen instantly — in fact, it may not happen at all if the stars are not aligning your way. My main problem when I first started trading was that not only were my glasses rose-coloured, they also had oversized horse blinkers attached to the sides. It didn't even cross my mind that owning a small business could be hard work (compared with motherhood and swimming), nor that it wouldn't be an instant success. I do blame the whole 'no job before starting a business' situation. Having success, and being able to feel secure in relation to the eventual running of your small business, requires both patience and time. Don't be too concerned or stressed if customers aren't waiting on the doorstep the moment your business starts trading. Give yourself and your business a chance to gain the momentum it deserves. In my pre-trading days, I set up information booths at the shopping centre to advertise and inform the public about the swim school opening. We advertised that we would be taking bookings from our booth near the food court from 9 a.m. to 12 p.m. on certain days. The first day was a complete fizzer and we only had 55 families enrol. I was concerned because we had projected that it would require at least 850 families to break even. By the second day, the word had obviously passed around and we added an extra 180 families to our books.

I hope things are instant for you, but I urge you to stay focused and positive if things don't immediately start moving onward and upward. It took us a good six months after opening to get the numbers we needed — and that was just to break even. Try not to stress. It's difficult in that first year to project trends and flows within the business. By your second year you should be in a better position financially and you can begin to set some concrete goals.

Keep in mind that the attitude or mind-set you wake up with each morning will set the tone for the day. It will be virtually impossible to remain upbeat every day unless you live in 'business heaven' (which may exist for some, but for the majority, we exist in 'business reality').

Negative attitude = Waste of a day
Positive attitude = A productive day

Goal questionnaire

Setting clear, realistic and achievable goals for yourself and for your business will help set you on the road to success. Honesty is the key: be truthful about the energy you're prepared to put in, and step by step, goal by goal, you'll begin to see the results.

1. What small goal would you like to achieve when you begin your business?

2. What major goal would you like to achieve when you begin your business?

3. Have you set a goal in the past that you haven't achieved? If so, what contributed to it not being successful? What could you have done differently?

4. Have you set a goal in the past that was successful? If so, what was the reason behind it being successful?

5. How important are goals to you?

If you've never set yourself a goal, now is the time to start. Begin by looking at the goal you're trying to achieve and then break it down into smaller parts, each with a realistic timeframe attached. Rome wasn't built in a day and dreams generally aren't reached in 24 hours either. It's also a good idea to reward yourself along the way when small goals have been reached. In my experience, I found that once I began rewarding myself with small treats when little victories were met, it encouraged me to create even greater goals for myself — the greater the goal, the greater the reward. It not only gives you a sense of accomplishment and self-worth, but it slowly starts to wear down the 'negative little voices' in your head that may call from the sidelines every so often when tough times hit. Some people are born optimists and I'm sure that a positive outlook helps create success. I also believe that owning a small business is not for everyone and you certainly should do some serious soul-searching before you make a major commitment.

Healthy goals

Remember: maintaining good health is an important business goal as well. I know I've touched on this already, but don't let your health suffer because you're 'too busy' to look after yourself. Your business cannot go smoothly or operate efficiently without your good health and general well-being. When you are creating your business plan or weekly work schedule, make sure you factor in something active. It need only be 30 minutes every few days when the business is setting up, but I can tell you from experience that you'll feel a whole lot better and your business will feel the benefits.

As I've mentioned, one of my fitness goals was to run a half marathon. I gave myself six months of gradual running, but I had to sit down and work out how I was going to fit it into my work schedule and, of course, around my family. The only way I could fit running into my daily schedule was to get up and run before everyone else woke up. I've never been a 'runner' before — in fact, my body just isn't made for running — so it was quite a strain on my poor old knees to pound the pavement. Nevertheless, because I love setting goals and achieving them (or getting kind of close), it was far more achievable when I had planned my fitness goal around my business and family commitments.

To cut a long story short, I did the half marathon and was able to work my fitness regime around my work and family life. I certainly feel a lot more energised for it. Thankfully, when I got the hosting job on *TBL*, I was actually quite fit from the all the running I'd been doing. I was quite unaware of the amount of energy required to host a television show on a daily basis, and the fact that I had managed to stay fit and healthy was my saving grace.

If you are not big on exercise or eating well, now is the time to start a new health and fitness regime for the sake of your business. There's no reason you can't juggle both. It must be on the very top of your list of priorities.

As a business owner, setting mini and major goals will become a standard part of your overall plan for success. A great way to manage goals and think through new and innovative ways to enhance your business is by getting out and exercising. Being cooped up in an office or a workplace can sometimes stifle your ability to make good decisions or come up with creative and fresh ideas to boost the attractiveness of your product or service. Getting out into the fresh air, going for a brisk walk or jog, riding a bike or just going for a swim really kick-starts endorphin production, the 'feel good' chemicals in your brain. If exercise and a good diet are already part of your life, then you've probably already experienced that exercise and healthy eating make you feel more alert and alive at work.

If fitness just isn't a part of your daily or weekly regime and you want it to be, then write down the small goals you want to achieve before you get started. Here's a simple template for you:

Day of the week	Weight (kg)	Exercise goal	Exercise completed	Overall feeling
Monday	65.5	Run 8 km	6 km	Very sluggish
Tuesday	65.3	Run 4 km Walk 4 km	8 km	Right knee hurting
Wednesday	66	Run 10 km	10 km	Angry — had takeaway for dinner
Thursday	65.5	Walk 8 km	6 km	Not bad

I use my diary to write down what I do on a daily basis. If I have an ocean race or fun run coming up, I generally count down to the day from a month out and then note down my goals for the days leading up to the event. For example, four weeks from a half marathon I would set my weekly running goal at 50 kilometres for the week; three weeks out it would decrease to 40 kilometres, and so on. My business goals are written down in the same fashion. January will start with a projected monthly earning of _____, advertising spending is _____ and so on.

Many of you probably already set goals without even realising it. Taking a few minutes out of your day to write down what you hope to achieve on a weekly or monthly basis, whether it be with your family, health or work, will open up a world of positive thinking you may not have known existed. I guarantee that you'll find qualities within yourself that you didn't know you had. And, hey, if you set a goal and don't achieve it, you probably know where you went wrong and how you can improve anyway. Writing a specific goal on paper makes it more genuine and valid — you've made a solid commitment to achieve something. It's almost officially committing yourself to an idea — kind of like when you sign your name on your wedding day to say that you've committed yourself to your new spouse! At the risk of sounding corny, I love making goals that I don't tell anyone about. It feels like I'm going about my daily business hiding a special secret: something that I'm aiming towards.

Set your goals and take aim at your targets with relentless purpose. And, while you're at it, you might just get fit too. Your personal health and the health and well-being of your business are sure to benefit.

My little tips

- Write down your goals, big and small, and remember to keep a daily journal or diary of your progress. This is a great way to keep track of things and it will spur you on if things slow down in the development department.

- Take charge of your attitude and focus 100 per cent on your goals.
- Keep goals to yourself. Don't let the whole world know what you intend to achieve.
- Don't let anyone change your goals through their negativity.
- Reward yourself when a goal is reached. If you are not big on rewarding yourself, still take the opportunity to pat yourself on the back and feel good.
- Don't beat yourself up if a goal isn't met. Learn from your mistakes and move on. Re-evaluate the situation as to why the goal wasn't reached.
- Surround yourself with positive people who encourage you to achieve your goals.
- Visualise only good things happening.
- Think about how you will feel when your goals are achieved.
- Stay optimistic. Remember: the glass is ALWAYS half full.

The Business Plan

What is a business plan?

A business plan is a model based around the business, which is usually prepared before the business begins trading. It can be as basic or comprehensive as you like, but generally your business plan will include important background information and specific strategies, as well as your personal goals for the future of the business. Many small business owners become a little daunted by the prospect of writing a business plan — and rightly so! In some cases, it may seem like you're about to embark on a 10,000-word essay for school, which you know will then be dissected upon completion by your teacher. Others revel in the prospect of getting their teeth into a thoroughly researched and well-documented plan that leaves no business projection or stone unturned. In all honesty, you can create a business plan that is as simple or as well researched as you wish, but the bottom line is ... you must have one! Even if you have already secured the financial side of your business, preparing and completing a business plan is like creating a blueprint for your future business success.

You probably already have business goals in mind and where you hope to see the business progressing in years to come. Having these goals and future projections as part of your business plan can be a vital tool in helping you to achieve them. In general terms, seeing your ideas and dreams written down on a business plan is like cementing them into something you can touch. You will always keep your initial business plan (and it will become an important piece of history when you go on to be a small business mogul!) and you can use it as a guide for any future businesses that you start up.

I still refer to my original business plan with a great deal of pride. It helps me recognise the abundance of knowledge and experience I've gained along the way and how much my business sense has developed from those initial planning stages. I also spend some time every six months upgrading and adding to my plan to stay current. Your business plan shouldn't be viewed as a document that you draw up before the business starts, only then to be left in a desk drawer, never again to see the light of day. Try to revise it on a consistent basis, altering sections (for example marketing, goals and finance) that need to stay current.

Your plan should be a personal documentation or vision for your business and its eventual future success. If you're the organised type, then the business model will have an almost cathartic effect for you. If you're the opposite, then the structure will come as a welcome relief. Many of you may have already started the research section for your business plan without even realising it. The 'idea' itself, the proposed location and your own personal financial goals are all crucial aspects of the plan. Doing thorough research for your plan also makes you consider areas you may not have thought important. Neglecting specifics could unfortunately mean the sudden demise of your dream because you simply didn't expect it. You need to be prepared for all possibilities.

Your business plan is also your detailed back-up strategy. You would never go on a family trip or holiday without planning where you were going to eat/sleep/stop/visit, and the same applies to a business. The fastest way to your business dying a death is through lack of preparation and planning. With a well-researched business plan you'll never be left in the dark.

Getting down to business

Always keep in mind who you're writing your business plan for. Ultimately, it will always be a useful reference tool throughout the running of your business, but you may also need it for the following people or institutions:

- **Bank manager** It will always help you to get finance from banking institutions if you have a plan to support your business idea. It will be necessary to have all of your financial information and history, but to have a prepared business plan to support your 'financials' can only help you get support.
- **Investor** Having a well-researched plan in place will increase your chances of gaining an investor. If they can see a business plan it will only cement in their minds that you are serious about the future of your business.
- **New partner** If the business requires a partner, the business plan will certainly be beneficial when showing any potential partners your projections and plans for the future. Often, a new partner may only be coming on board to support your business dream from a financial perspective, so seeing on paper where you intend heading will be crucial to that support and understanding.
- **You** It's always handy to have a plan that allows you to see and project where your profits will be going. Starting a new business can be daunting, but having a business plan in place will help reinforce your ideas and goals. It's like having your own road map to a destination that hasn't yet been discovered — only positive things can come from preparing one.

Where to start

Back in the 'olden days' when I was doing my business plan, it had to be this massive compilation of facts and figures, jam-packed with information that may never be referred to or required. It wasn't that much different to those ridiculously long and tedious assignments you'd get from your teacher on a subject that you were never going to need in the real world! It was no great wonder that so many aspiring young entrepreneurs took the easy path and bypassed 'business plan avenue' (or 'tedious avenue', for want of a better name). Not these days, however. Some smart person — probably some entrepreneurial mother of five with limited time, good organisational skills and fantastic time management — realised that the world was changing and no one had the time or patience to read a huge folder full of numbers and projections. Instead, they prepared a simple business plan template for the 21st-century entrepreneur and now there are hundreds of simple and easy-to-follow programs that can be tailored to your needs. You don't have to be a great researcher or planner, but the more time and effort you put into the construction of your plan, the more benefits will flow to your business.

Template time

There are lots of computer programs and internet sites that provide business plan templates and advice. They're bound to make your life a whole lot easier. Take a look at these:

- **www.business.gov.au** I've already mentioned this site in Chapter 1 because it gives a wonderful overview of the small business world, but it has so many features that will just blow you away. The business plan template is readily available to download and then you simply fill in the required fields. It's a comprehensive model that helps you put together a concise business plan from start to finish.

- **www.australiansmallbusiness.com.au** This site has fantastic business plan software and books to purchase online.
- **www.anz.com/small-business** This is the ANZ Bank's site and you'll find a range of comprehensive resources and tools to take you through creating a plan from the bottom up. Most of the major banks have similar online resources. The Bank of Queensland (www.boq.com.au) also has an easy-to-follow template in PDF form.

There's great computer software available also, which outlines everything you could possibly want to know about writing a comprehensive and well-documented business plan. Simply go to any of our major computer and office-based stores, for example Officeworks or Harvey Norman, and browse through the options.

Constructing a plan from scratch

Completing your business plan and seeing it all bound up in a folder will not only bring you some comfort but will give you peace of mind as well. Holding that document in your hand reinforces that you are not embarking on an impetuous idea, but instead forging ahead with an organised and well-thought-out venture.

Your business plan is the result of all the homework and study you've put into your potential business idea. This is what it should include:

1. A summary and detailed description of your business
- This should pack a serious punch. Briefly yet passionately outline your vision, especially if you're trying to attract potential investors or persuade a not-so-eager spouse.
- Thoroughly describe the business — the products or services you're selling or providing; your potential customer base; what makes your business unique.

2. Your qualifications
- Outline your qualifications and work experience in your business area. Include licences, certificates, courses, seminars, etc.
- Provide a brief summary of other aspects of your background that would help you run a successful business. Experience in a different area can demonstrate dedication, skill and business prowess.

3. Your customer base
- Do a profile of your potential customers — age, demographic, gender, etc. This section will be the key to the success of your business — no customers, no business!

4. Your competitors
- Give a detailed outline of your competitors and their proximity to your proposed business.
- List the number of competitors that are offering the same or similar services or products in your proposed location.
- Do an overall assessment of your competitors' strengths and weaknesses. What sets you apart from them? If they were to expand and diversify, how would this affect your business?

5. Your location
- Give an assessment of your chosen location and why it melds conveniently and appropriately with surrounding stores and clientele. (See the location section in Chapter 9.)
- Explain the demographic of the area and why it fits with your business concept, for example a large number of young families moving in, employment opportunities have increased in the area, etc.
- Give descriptions of other businesses in your location, especially those that are doing well.

6. Your marketing, advertising and promotions strategy
- Outline how and where you will market your business.
- State the amount of capital (money) you will require to market and advertise your business. Break it

down into 'Initial' and 'Ongoing' categories. Provide realistic figures on your budgeted cash flow when it comes to initial and ongoing marketing and advertising.

- If you're creating your own marketing methods, give a few examples of your concepts, such as add-on offers to encourage repeat business (spend over $100 and receive a $25 gift voucher), customer competitions with prizes on offer, or regular sales to increase numbers through the door.

7. Your finance

- If you've already secured finance, state the provider or the source. If you haven't yet secured finance, list the financial institutions that you will approach.
- Create a brief summary of the current market conditions for your proposed business.
- Provide profit/loss and cash-flow forecasts. An accountant, financial planner or a friend experienced in business can help you here if you're feeling out of your depth.
- Provide monthly and yearly projections. Again, get some help from an accountant, financial planner or friend experienced in business if you need to.

8. Your business structure

- State whether you will be a sole trader, a partnership, a family business, a company or a trust.

- Give a detailed outline of the desired structure of your business. For example, will you be the manager as well as the owner? How many staff do you expect to have? A sample structure could be:

```
Owner/Manager (you)
         ⇩
  Assistant Manager
   ⇩          ⇩
 Casual      Casual
```

9. The general running of the business

- Give contact details for your accountant and/or bookkeeper.
- State any initial equipment required and show costings.
- State your cash-flow requirements.
- Show that all legal requirements are in place, including licences, permits, etc. For example, my swim school staff all had Swim Australia certification (or equivalent) as well as CPR certification and Blue Cards, which meant they could work with children. This not only meant that all my staff were fully qualified and trained instructors, but that I could register my school with Swim Australia.

10. Insurance

- Outline the coverage you have and show the premiums you will pay. Make sure you thoroughly research the insurance policy you take out and that it suits your business. Insurance can sometimes seem costly but it's too risky not to have it. Make sure you shop around. This is definitely not an area where you want 'dodgy brothers' coverage.

11. Your mission statement and goals

- You can be as bold as you like in this section. Make sure you assemble realistic short- and long-term goals and projections for your business. An enthusiastic and passionate mission statement can give your business plan a genuine boost when it's submitted to a bank to help secure a loan.

My business plan

Looking at my business plan circa 2002, it embarrassingly resembles something from the Dark Ages. I was one of those business plan 'pooh-poohers', who thought the very idea of spending valuable time writing and researching something that was only a 'plan' (especially when we had already secured finance for the business) seemed like a complete waste of energy. Upon meeting with a fellow swim school owner to discuss current trends within the industry, my helpful friend asked:

'You *have* done a business plan, haven't you?'

I casually looked sideways at my husband who rolled his eyes as if to convey the words *I told you it was important!* without actually saying them.

'Yeah ... it's, um, still under construction,' I replied, clearly fibbing through my teeth.

Of course, when someone other than your spouse mentions the importance of something, you finally decide to get your butt into gear.

I'll admit I was a little apprehensive to start a business plan given my history of not preparing for anything (except in the pool). Things got even scarier when my research revealed the extent of what I was getting myself into. There were aspects of owning and operating a small business that I didn't even know existed. Tax and superannuation issues, bottom lines, policies and procedures — the list went on and on. You would think, given the fact that I had been so unsuccessful and ill-prepared with past business ventures, that this time I'd be more savvy. I simply thought that I could build a swimming pool in a major shopping centre, hire some swim instructors and the customers would flock to the business like the scene from the closing credits of the amazing and inspiring film *Field of Dreams,* starring Kevin Costner. I literally thought, 'If I build it they will come.'

If you're an optimistic business entrepreneur and you haven't seen this movie, do yourself a favour and hire it. You'll love the ending and I hope it will be an inspiration for when you eventually open your own business.

It would be a fair assessment to say that the entire time I'd spent preparing and researching my business plan, I'd also been unwittingly educating myself. The biggest eye-opener was the importance of cash flow and how it could make or break a business. Sure, I knew that I couldn't run the business without money, but what I hadn't realised was the detrimental effect the actions of other people can have on your flourishing business. Basically, you depend on others to make payments to you in order for your business to stay afloat. I couldn't help but wonder if I was going to be able to cope with the concept of having to rely on other people. And what if unexpected costs popped up that you hadn't budgeted for — what then? I really had absolutely no idea about the amount of money I was going to need to secure my business and keep it healthily afloat. I assumed that if I had X amount of money in my account and I knew exactly what my monthly outgoings were, then surely things would all be fine and dandy. WRONG! The business plan made me realise that unforeseen and costly issues happened from time to time and my bank balance needed to be well and truly ready for that possibility.

The key to your success and peace of mind is knowing every little aspect of the day-to-day running of your business, and your business plan will help you realise this. I made a costly mistake during the initial years of trading when I knew very little about my business. My bookkeeper and a staff member managed the books, and frankly the whole thing baffled me. I was having my second child and I simply didn't have the time to devote to bookwork. I am embarrassed and astonished when I think back to how little I knew about my own business. I couldn't even tell you our monthly rent, let alone how much money we had in the bank. Our doors were still open, so that must have meant things were going OK, surely?

It was only after the first year when our silent partner kept calling each month to see the figures did I start to think — yes, what *are* the figures? When I realised we were going backwards at a rapid pace, I finally decided to start taking a bit more notice. What a difference that made!

I managed to cut costs dramatically while maintaining the same high-quality service we'd been providing for our customers. Almost instantly, things started looking a heck of a lot more promising. To this very day, I can tell you every outgoing cost and expense my business requires per month down to the last cent. This may take a year or so to see with a clearly outlined spreadsheet, but knowing everything you can about the expenses of your business is crucial to having longevity as a business owner.

Mind your business

- Purchase easy-to-follow software or download a simple template to assist you.
- Research every topic thoroughly — don't leave a stone unturned.
- Don't become too over-the-top with future projections. Put realistic goals into play instead.
- Be upfront from a financial point of view if your business plan is going to be presented to potential investors.
- Size doesn't always matter when it comes to your business plan. It should be as concise as you need it to be. You can always keep adding to it along the way.

Business plan questionnaire

Now that I have shown the positive aspects of preparing a business plan, if you are still in two minds as to whether to put your energies into one, here is a simple questionnaire to help you make up your mind.

1. Do you think the business plan is an important part of planning for your new business?

2. How much time are you willing to spend on your business plan?

3. What is the main reason for constructing your business plan?

4. If you've decided that a business plan is irrelevant, have you looked at other ways to get yourself organised and structured?

My little tips

- A business plan is not imperative, but it will at the very least get you asking questions and researching areas you may not have thought of.
- Think of the business plan as your personal road map to the end destination — success.
- A business plan is also a great tool for reassessing your goals for the business.
- Business plans can be as simple or comprehensive as you like — just don't put the whole idea into the too-hard basket.
- Make sure your business and staff have all the necessary permits and licences.

Getting the Word Out

My foray into marketing and advertising

I had just started building my swim school at a shopping centre in Brisbane, and just as soon as the concrete was being poured, the pool builders were finding advertising and marketing paraphernalia under the door seeking my business. I had a budget in mind for advertising but no real idea about how best to use the funds for a comprehensive marketing promotion. It staggered me to realise how fast people can track a new business down even before the front door is opened. Given some of the cover letters I received, I'm certain most companies thought I had money to burn, considering their fee structures and plans outlining my future advertising costs and what they had in store for me. Suddenly, my little swim school, which was quite literally just laying down its foundations, became a honey pot for advertising agencies and marketing gurus. With absolutely zero per cent business knowledge or experience in any type of business promotion, I was still smart enough to look at my budget and work out that the advertising would be very modest and affordable at the start.

I did have a little chuckle to myself one day close to opening when a major cinema advertising company gave me a lovely and courteous call requesting we meet for a coffee and chat about the possibility of advertising my business on the big screen. I was curious, more than anything else, and I even allowed myself to take a moment to imagine my modest business being promoted at a movie theatre. Needless to say, the dream promptly came crashing down when the consultant revealed the base advertising costs. At the time (and still to this day), advertising in a cinema just doesn't come close to suiting my budget.

After opening your business, you will find that phone calls and letters from various advertising companies and marketing outlets will pursue you with vigour. It's now nine years on and I still receive at least two calls per week from various companies offering different ways to 'promote and enhance your business'. My advice is always stick to your budget and be open to any ideas that come your way. Advertising is such a tricky, costly and sometimes problematic area for all business owners. It's a bit of a budget gamble at times to know where to outlay the money for advertising and marketing in order to get the most impact.

Basically, do your homework. Chances are pretty high that you already know where best to spend your money to promote your business. It's always a good idea to ask around and do some research before you decide where to start spending on advertising. Be mindful that sometimes you have to invest in professional help to assist you in areas that aren't your forte.

Early on, when I was doing letterbox drops at day-care centres, I attempted (very poorly) to create the design myself for the postcard-size advertisements. Bad idea! I am not a graphic designer nor do I have the appropriate software to create gorgeous, eye-catching images, so it was more beneficial for me to get a designer to create them for me. If you know what you want, or have a general idea of colours and layout, then a designer will most probably create your exact concept. If you are really lucky, they will generate an image or concept that far exceeds your expectations (and anything you would ever be able to produce yourself). This is without doubt money very well spent. You'll also find that often a designer will be part of the overall package with the printing.

You don't need a massive budget

Within the swim school industry, you can register with an amazing organisation called Swim Australia. Launched in 1997, its mission is to promote Australian swimming and increase awareness of the benefits of learning to swim in a safe and enjoyable way. It also hopes to keep Australians swimming throughout their lives. Every year Swim Australia has a conference and awards night for all the registered swim schools in Australia. A few of those awards encompass the area of advertising and marketing. The first year I attended I was completely blown away by the design concepts and marketing techniques of some of the award winners, many of which were just average swim schools on a tight budget. It did make me realise how smart I needed to be with my budget and how you don't need to be a McDonald's or a Harvey Norman to enhance your business with the right ideas to promote your business. It's more a matter of being as creative and innovative as possible in order to stand out in your particular field.

What is marketing?

Marketing basically involves recognising your potential customer base and promoting the particular products or services you're providing to those consumers. Remember when you were in the research phase of your planning and you were gathering important information and data in relation to your competitors? This is a major part of the marketing process. Researching the fee you charge your customers for your products or services is all part of marketing. Finding out as much information about your potential customers or 'potential market for business' is also marketing. A marketing company provides all these services, and their job would be to give you as much valuable data, information and statistics about your clients as possible. They would include information on who your potential clients are, where you should advertise and exactly where your customers are now shopping. There would also be information about the prices and/or level of service they are receiving from your competitors. These marketing gurus would be compiling all sorts of different data that you may not have even considered.

Marketing and advertising — what's the difference?

It's perfectly natural to put both marketing and advertising under one banner because they go hand in hand with one another. Certainly, if you have been working for an employer your whole life, you may not have needed to experience either one. Once again, as women I think we're pretty switched on when it comes to knowing our potential market and where to advertise. Most new business owners won't have the budget to take on a professional advertising or marketing company. It would be nice and very handy, though, wouldn't it? When I was at the marketing stage with my business, we had a close friend in public relations who quoted us a considerable amount of money to market and promote our business. She had put together an impressive package that really blew us away, but her fees were unrealistic compared with our conservative budget. However, using a company or specific person to handle the marketing side of the business does free up a lot of time to concentrate on more important areas of your business planning. Oh, to have a bottomless pit of money! I certainly knew my limited capabilities, but I used some initiative and imagination and got things started myself. Honestly, if I handled things without using a professional, you most certainly can too. It comes down to having some confidence in yourself to do the best job you can within your allotted budget.

Gathering your information

Marketing your business idea might seem like a drag, especially if you don't like asking questions, researching or making calls. Knowing what I do now, I think marketing is a relevant and significant means of gathering as much information as you can before starting out in business. I also know how time-consuming it can be. You can skip the marketing stage if you like, but my advice is to factor it into your planning hours — your business plan will most definitely require it anyway, and so will a potential investor or loans officer. Look at it as an important way to find out about your competitors and where potential customers may be hiding out.

If you're starting out in an area that's unfamiliar, you'll probably need to do some heavy-duty marketing. I hate talking on the phone, so if you're anything like me find someone who loves it, or invest in a marketing company to do the initial calling for you. It will definitely be money well spent. If you are watching your pennies and would prefer not to do the market research yourself, you can always prepare your own survey and get someone else with a personable manner to conduct the survey on your behalf. A hands-on approach is often needed so that a business owner becomes acquainted with potential customers. It's time to put your fears aside and make customer service and consumer marketing a top priority. This can only enhance your business because you'll be asking the questions and getting important feedback from future customers in return.

You've got to ask the right questions to get the most helpful marketing data. The more you know about the business you're entering, the more successful you'll be at finding (and keeping) the right customers — and eventually making the all-important sales.

Marketing and advertising questionnaire

Marketing and advertising are important elements in setting up a business. Doing thorough research could save money and angst in the long run. Ask yourself these essential questions:

1. Do you have a niche product and market? Does your product or service fill a need or assist people? Can you appeal to a cross-section within your market by highlighting different aspects of your product? How does your product compare with others?

2. Should the price of your product/service be lower than the competition, or should you charge a higher price to enhance your product's perceived value? Is your pricing adequate to meet profit expectations? Is the location of your business charging relevant prices compared to the demographic?

3. Who are your potential customers? Where do they live? How much money do they make?

4. Who are your biggest competitors? What are they doing to create amazing businesses? What are they doing wrong? How can you do things better?

5. What type of medium (newspaper, letterbox drop, radio, etc.) will you use to advertise? How will you measure the results of your promotions? Will you do it all yourself?

6. How will you best deliver your product/service to the customer? Will you offer a guarantee? How will you handle complaints? Will you give people their money back if they are dissatisfied?

Collecting useful data

So, where are you going to find useful information and data for your particular market? If you're not using a marketing company to do this for you, then the job can be daunting. Here are some great starting points:

- **Discussion Groups** Get together with others in your chosen business field for an inside look at the market. Joining an active forum will help you spot trends, determine attitudes among market observers and provide you with an avenue to make contacts for research and product development. This is the perfect way to gather business contacts and remain in the loop. There's nothing worse than people within the industry knowing important stuff/trends/new products while you've been completely left in the dark. Stay across as much of the market as possible.

- **Internet search requests** You can get a snapshot of the key words people are using on internet search engines within your product or service. This lets you examine how often a phrase is used and the competition for those expressions. You can use online services such as those provided by Yahoo and Google.

- **Trade publications** Subscribe to magazines and newspapers within your target market. Not only is this a great way to keep up with current market conditions, but you'll also stay in the loop as your business matures. It's also the perfect opportunity to see how your competitors are marketing and advertising products and the different methods they are using to 'woo' potential customers.

- **Blogs and websites** Hello 21st century! Blogs and websites are an amazing way to keep track of your competition. They allow you to keep abreast with competitors' upcoming sales, product and service fees, and customer service. Some websites even have a 'testimonials' page where you can read satisfied customers' feedback. With blogs, contributors give you a glimpse into what readers and subscribers are interested in and what they're commenting on, which is a great insight into the market.

If your budget allows ...

Calling in the marketing gurus to do the job can be a good move, especially if you've got the budget for it but not much time or energy. It may also give you a broader insight into your market and therefore it's a sound investment. There is a multitude of great marketing companies right around Australia, but here is one on the internet that may be helpful:

- **Marketing Angels — www.marketingangels.com.au:** this company offers very cost-effective, do-it-yourself marketing programs as well as comprehensive assistance within all areas of marketing through workshops, e-guides and private marketing coaching. They also offer small group marketing workshops in some states where you work closely with a marketing consultant. This is definitely worth every penny and the information and knowledge that you learn in a short time is priceless. Some of the topics covered in the seminars include a review of marketing opportunities and goals; maximising marketing activities; marketing challenges and ways to overcome them; and setting marketing goals/actions.

Using a professional company or investing in a half-day workshop can be invaluable. Let's face it — unless you've done a marketing degree, chances are you won't know where to begin without a little bit of help from trained professionals. A workshop or seminar may also give you the opportunity to brainstorm with other small business owners starting up their own marketing plans.

DIY marketing

When you're starting out, it's difficult and often downright impossible to predict how much you're going to spend on advertising. I had an annual budget that I wanted to stick to each year, but sometimes I was forced to spend a few extra dollars that I didn't necessarily have floating about. Remember, it's not the size of your budget that matters, but the way you use it. My initial budget was $2,000 for the first year. That equated to just under $38.50 per week — a tiny amount considering most of us would spend $40 a week on things we don't really need. I used every last available cent, but I was creative with it. One thing that I would have done was advertise my business on my car. I was driving my car quite a few kilometres every day, but I just didn't want my name on the side of it. If my business was called Bubbles Swim School, for instance, I would have jumped at the chance. Mobile advertising can be costly upfront, but then you have it for life — or for the life of your car, at least.

I've found that every so often I'll have to think outside the box in order to stand out from my competitors. I am fortunate to be in a high-traffic area, but when I was first starting out, I had to find innovative ways to get my business stuck in the minds of potential customers, while still keeping the budget down (not the easiest thing to achieve). I find that it's also a great idea to look outside your industry or product market for inspiration. Make sure you make note of any advertising methods that stand out to you. It's an extremely competitive and tough game in most areas of business, so pioneering ways to entice new customers is really important.

More dash than cash

You probably have a good idea already about the best way to advertise your business. Recently, I was in search of a personal-training-cum-boot-camp group to join over the winter months. These days, there seems to be so many of them around and it becomes quite easy to be confused by who is offering the best deals and services. I eventually joined one purely by accident. I was ordering a coffee at my local café and perched in the corner, on one of those swivelling advertising stands, was a business card for a local training group. On the back of the card was a complete weekly training schedule and the prices. Before

I knew it I was enrolled and attending the following day's session. Here's my point: these businesses don't advertise in lavish and expensive ways. They think outside the box and strategically place advertising material in high-traffic locations — cafés are probably foolproof.

I tend only to advertise in the local paper or in children's magazines for the swim school, where I know my potential customers (that is, parents) are. In the early days of my business, I travelled to more than a hundred day-care centres in the area, delivering brochures to go directly into the children's pockets at the centres. If they brought that brochure along to the opening day, they received 10 per cent off their swimming fees. On that day we had 286 parents take up this special offer, so it was well and truly worthwhile promoting it. If you give your customers a great gift or incentive to buy your product or use your service, chances are higher that they will give you a go.

Not all of us trade in high-traffic positions, so businesses that are off the beaten track may need to find novel ways to advertise and entice prospective customers. Here are some inventive suggestions:

- **Day-care centre pocket drops** A colourful, double-sided postcard-size advertisement should reel them in. This can be quite a cost-effective way to market your business, especially if you make an order for a bulk print. Remember to 'hook' them with a special offer and make the advertisement as bright as possible.
- **Letterbox drops** You can do this yourself and it's great exercise as well. Make sure your brochure or advertising material doesn't look like junk mail, otherwise it will just

get tossed away. I love the postcard-size advertisements
— for some reason I am less inclined to throw them away.
When I see really beautifully designed ones in cafés and
shops, I take them home to see what they are advertising.

- **Local newspapers** City-wide papers charge higher
advertising fees than local newspapers. Sure, the
circulation isn't as wide, but chances are your target
market is within your immediate area. Your aim should
be to grab as many potential customers as possible, but
advertising can be very expensive in major print and
media. Start small and then, when the budget allows,
you can broaden your range to reach a wider audience.

- **Magazines** There's a variety of magazines at
newsagencies that may be specific to your industry or
clientele. It's a good idea to check their advertising costs
— if it fits within your budget, go for it. Remember
to attach a special offer. Other magazines are free of
charge to your customers but you incur the advertising
costs. You'll often find these in doctors' surgeries, day-
care centres, coffee shops and even swim schools, and
they're a great way to advertise.

- **Brochures and business cards** This is a great
distribution method for any business. You can basically
include anything you want. Make sure it's eye-catching,
otherwise it will blend in with all the other brochures
on the stand. Coffee shops are also great venues for this
type of promotional material, especially if they have a
stand available and customers can browse while they're
waiting for their takeaway. Take note of the coffee shops
or other traders that distribute brochures and cards for
other businesses.

- **Radio and cinema advertising** Chances are you don't quite have the budget at the moment to consider radio or cinema advertising. Don't get too despondent, however, as not many small business owners do. On the other hand, if you have a granny with a pocketful of cash she's willing to throw your way, then you've got nothing to lose. Make sure the advertising reaches the correct demographic for your product or service.

- **Yellow Pages** This 'tome' has been around for as long as I can remember and it can certainly be a cost-effective way to advertise. Even with the internet connected throughout our house, I still grab the *Yellow Pages* for most services I need. There is something uniquely comforting about looking in a big book with everything there in front of me for comparison. It's often faster to get the ol' *Yellow Pages* out and 'let your fingers do the walking', rather than wait for the internet to start up. There's a range of different advertising options on offer. Call 13 23 78, or go to www.yellowpages.com.au. You can list your business for free through the *Yellow Pages* website, but be prepared to pay to include more information or images. Check out your competitors' advertisements and make it your mission to be more appealing to your potential customers.

- **Internet marketing** Many small business owners find internet marketing more affordable. Google AdWords and Yahoo! Search Marketing are two trendy options for getting small business products or services across to potential internet customers.

- **Good ol' word of mouth** Nothing beats this as a marketing strategy. News travels fast these days and it doesn't take much for two people to be having a conversation about a great coffee shop they've just visited or the shocking mess of a haircut they've just received at a new salon. Word of mouth is generally spontaneous and is achieved by businesses through merit (or demerit, as the case may be) without any form of strategy.

- **Customer referrals** Many small and medium-sized businesses around local neighbourhoods use referral marketing. It relies on gaining new customers by referrals, usually through word of mouth. By creating a positive impression on one of your satisfied customers, they too can benefit from referring a potential customer. For example, refer a friend and receive a 25 per cent discount on your next purchase/treatment/service.
- **Press, news or media releases** So, your business may not be the hottest thing in town just yet, but local radio stations, newspapers or journalists are always looking for local stories to write or talk about. Not every day is a big news day and often media outlets are on the lookout for fresh material. All they need from you is a 'hook'. Give them a really interesting reason to want to cover the opening of your new business. This can often come at absolutely no cost to you. Remember, sometimes you need to put yourself out there to be noticed, plus you have absolutely nothing to lose and everything to gain by being bold.
- **Car advertising** This is another cost-effective way to advertise. It's important to keep your car in great shape — if it's a little worse for wear, potential customers my think it reflects the state of your business. If it's not your personal car but is driven by an employee, insist

the appearance and standard of driving is high. You don't want a car recklessly zooming around the streets with your business name splashed all over it. Keep the design simple — it's easier for potential customers to read the contact information and remember your business.

- **Uniforms and promotional clothing** This, in some ways, is similar to car advertising — as employees are walking around in their lunchbreak, they're advertising the company. Don't overcapitalise, though. One big mistake was going too bold and expensive with our uniform at the swim school. The instructors and staff had quite expensive shirts with our logo screen-printed on the front. After just a few washes, the shirts either shrank and/or lost their colour. I had spent so much money and hadn't even taken the time to check the durability on the care label. The school became really humid after about 30 minutes, so the uniforms weren't suited to the climate either. Do your homework. Check out competitors that look fresh and professional in their work uniforms. Next time, I'm going with the same T-shirt manufacturers that make my son's school athletic clothing — it's tough, durable and just lasts and lasts.

- **Packaging** I love it when I go into a quaint boutique or gift store and they hand you your purchase in a gorgeous brown bag with a twisted straw handle and the store's logo or brand on the side. It's very 'old school', but it creates the feeling that you've purchased a unique item and not something generic from the big-name stores. Plastic bags don't say 'exclusive purchase' to me. If you have an internet-based business, then personalising the packaging will send that personal touch that most of us appreciate. I sometimes buy my yarn products from an internet business called The Wool Shack (www.thewoolshack.com). It's based in Perth and has amazing products coupled with wonderful customer service. The first time I placed an order, my yarn arrived promptly, it was neatly packed and attached to my receipt was a little bag of jelly beans. I know this seems insignificant, but it really was a delicate touch that personalised my order and gave me a feeling of being special. You might think I'm weird, but I've never been a materialistic person. I'm much more likely to get that warm-and-fuzzy feeling from something handmade than from something sleek, shiny and expensive. Whatever the reason, it still meant something to me and I always look for my jelly beans before inspecting my purchase. I think it made an impact because I wasn't expecting it. It's an example of the little things being important — for a small outlay, you may get a big return.

- **Blogs** I love a great blog. You can actually use blogs as a way to gather your market analysis without paying a cent. Many websites have blogs attached, but if you haven't got your website ready quite yet, you can still get your blog up and running without spending any money. Make sure you let your customers know about your blogs on your advertising material. Free blogs can be created at www.blogger.com and www.typepad.com.

- **Sponsorship** When my youngest son Kai started playing rugby union for the local club, they asked for sponsors to help out with purchasing the new team uniform. In this case, sponsorship offered the opportunity to advertise a business logo and design on the front of the jerseys; at the end of the season, all the players could keep the one they'd been wearing. If the team couldn't find a sponsor, the alternative was to play the season with club-owned jerseys and the kids had to hand them back at the end of the season. It really was a no-brainer for me. Kai wanted his own first rugby jersey anyway, and it allowed me to get my business logo visible for many potential customers. The price of the sponsorship was about the same as if I'd advertised in the local paper for a couple of weeks. The kudos and goodwill that were generated among the club and the other parents on the team were an added bonus as well. It really was a win–win situation for me as a parent and as a business owner.

Your marketing plan

Before you get started, sit down and fill out the sample marketing plan that follows to get you in the right frame of mind. Don't get all stressed or concerned if you still feel a little unsure of where to start or how to get the ball rolling. Marketing is a step-by-step process and it can seem a bit daunting when you are starting out. When your business is up and running, and you feel a bit more comfortable, the whole procedure will probably just fall into place. Some people, regardless of their budget, will focus on marketing their business with gusto and determination, and it's really up to you how much energy, money and time you put into marketing development. It's crucial not to become complacent when it comes to developing new ideas or strategies to keep your name up in lights. A marketing plan will assist you to focus on your marketing goals, your budget and your timeframe to get things ready for when you first start trading. There's nothing worse than being frazzled before you open. You're going to need all that energy to stay on top of things! Make sure you are organised with the timing of all your marketing ideas too. There's no use organising uniforms or advertising for the first day of trading a couple of days in advance. You need to be well and truly on top of everything before you open for business.

Sample marketing plan

What am I willing to spend per month/year to begin with?

- $50 per month

Will I create the marketing material yourself or use a professional — if so, what's the budget?

- Use a professional to create a logo for the business. My budget for the design process is $1,000.

Which medium will I use and what's the budget?

- Local newspapers to advertise the business opening — $850
- Brochures in letterboxes — $850 (I will deliver the material myself)
- Website — $2,000
- Car advertising — $1,000

What's my marketing timeline, based on my first day of trading?

- The business will open on Monday, 2 March 2012.
  Meet with the designer for logo in mid-January. Have brochures/business cards/postcard-size promotional material printed and designed by end of January. The business website should be designed and ready by mid-February. Car advertising to be completed by the end of February.

By this point, you've hopefully figured out that being organised is a major factor in the months before you start trading. Having a clear and concise plan of attack — one that's ready well ahead of time — will leave you more positive and less anxious about things. You don't need extra pressure at this stage.

A diary is a necessary part of life, in my experience. The only problem is that they aren't as visible as a wall-hanging or desk calendar. A small whiteboard at home and at your business is a good investment. It can be extremely handy to see a timeline of goals and tasks laid out before you.

If you are anything like me, I buy a new year paper diary around mid December with the intention of being very organised for the year ahead only to find I am no longer writing in it by mid March and once again I'm keeping notes in random books or simply on scraps of paper ... or heaven forbid, the back of my hand. For Christmas, my lovely husband bought me an iPad and this was my first opportunity to use an electronic gadget for a diary. I must say it has changed my life. The benefits of the electronic diary, whether it be an iPad, a computer itself or an electronic, palm-sized diary compared to the normal paper diary are:

- It reminds you of appointments without even going to the daily page.
- You simply type in any text, date, or someone's name and the organiser will find the entry you are looking for.
- There is no flicking through countless pages looking for phone numbers or messages you might have written for yourself months ago, everything is stored for you in the messages section.
- If you are using your computer as your daily organiser at your home office or business, your diary is right there sitting on your desk so it's easily accessible.

Of course, when using anything electronic, there are obvious downsides:

- losing data because you haven't backed up
- power failures
- waiting for the device to boot up
- cost
- you can't always fit your computer/iPad in your handbag.

Basically, the decision is up to you. You probably know by now what is going to work best for you, so stick to whatever keeps you as organised as possible.

Here's a sample calendar to get you started:

MARCH

Monday	Tuesday	Wednesday
	1 Meet designer	**2**
7	**8**	**9** Last day at the old job
14	**15**	**16**
21	**22** Merchant facility in	**23**
28	**29**	**30**

Thursday	Friday	Saturday	Sunday
3	**4** Store painted	**5**	**6**
10 Pick up office supplies	**11**	**12** Office equipment delivered 12 p.m.	**13**
17 Newspaper Advert in	**18**	**19**	**20**
24 Staff initiation	**25** **OPENING DAY**	**26**	**27**
31			

Mystery shoppers

Mystery shopping (using mystery consumers) is a tool used by market research companies to measure the quality of retail service or to gather specific information about products and services. Mystery shoppers pose as regular customers and perform specific tasks, such as purchasing a product, asking questions, registering complaints or behaving in a certain way. After they have collected enough information and formed an overall opinion of their experience, they then provide detailed feedback to the marketing company and or business owner. The marketing company reviews and analyses the information, completing an analysis report on the data for the client.

You can use these services to gauge the competency and overall standard of your employees and your business, especially if you can't be there 24/7. I've never used this method, mainly because a customer would let me know fairly quickly if my staff weren't helpful, positive and friendly. However, the swim school was nominated for a small business award a couple of years ago and I was informed that a 'mystery customer' would be visiting my school at some stage to assess my business on a variety of levels. The assessment would be based on:

- the time it took before they were served
- the general vibe within the swim school (positive or negative)
- the attitude and manner in which the staff member assisted them
- the amount of information they were given
- the types of products shown

- the staff member's willingness to answer questions and whether the answers were informative
- the cleanliness and appearance of the school
- the grooming of the staff
- the speed of service
- the overall vibe.

I wasn't all that nervous about the prospect of a mystery shopper. I'd owned the swim school for many years and rarely became rattled, even with customers, phones and screaming babies simultaneously vying for my attention. I'd learnt very early that the customer is always right and it caused much less stress if I dealt quickly and politely with the hard-to-please ones — even if it meant swallowing my pride sometimes. I was a little nervous, however, about the feedback I might get about my staff. I felt confident they would perform well, but there's nothing worse for a business owner than to find out that those fantastic staff members you've employed are actually conducting themselves in a negative and damaging manner. Well, we didn't win the award, but the mystery shopper's feedback was very positive and I felt I could breathe a little easier knowing that my staff conducted themselves in a positive and professional manner.

Check out these websites to find out more about mystery shoppers within Australia:
- www.mysteryshopper.com.au
- www.mysteryshopping.com.au
- www.australianfreepaidsurveys.com

Social networking

I'll be upfront and admit that when it comes to social networking I'm very much the amateur. Personally, I think the world has gone a little crazy in terms of online networking. When it's used in a positive and constructive manner, the social network can be a vital component of your business success. However, used in a negative manner it can spell disaster for your lifelong dream, so tread carefully.

I will admit to being a lover of websites and blogs, but Twitter, Facebook and other networking sites — forget it! I don't know if it's because I can't be bothered with something so time-consuming, or whether it's the technology that scares me. The negative press involved with social networking sites recently has stopped me even wanting to know anything about how they work. Even though I'm far from being a well-known person these days, I'm still a mother and a business owner, and I'd like to avoid being involved in something where my identity could be compromised. I did start a Facebook page purely out of curiosity and apparently I have six contacts that want to be my friends — what does this mean? Anyway, you get the picture. I'm no techno-wizard, but I do understand the positive value of social networking as a marketing tool for business. In fact, since I've done the research for this book, I'm half-convinced to give social networking a go again — when I have time to delve a little further!

Websites, blogs and tweets

I only learnt about the world of blogging by accident while purchasing a knitting book in a gift shop. The salesperson happened to have a bag of knitting behind her and we both started talking about different types of wool.

'You need to read this blog,' she firmly stated, while scribbling down the site.

'Is a blog something to do with a website?' I asked, not comfortable with the fact that a woman in her 60s was giving me a lesson in technology.

'Um ... kind of, but not really. You'll understand when you see it,' she comforted.

I promptly left the shop, drove home, and with my bag of purchases still hanging from my arm switched on my computer and started investigating this foreign world of 'blogging'. I was both gobsmacked and thrilled in one millisecond when the blog site lit up on my screen. How long had people been blogging and why was I oblivious to this creative online domain? It would be a huge understatement to admit that I was immediately hooked. It was like reading someone's diary but having permission to do so.

Blogging was totally guilt-free computer voyeurism into the daily lives of many of my favourite domestic goddesses. I'm a lover of all things crafty — knitting, crocheting, patchwork, cooking, gardening, you name it — and suddenly I was reading all about upcoming books to be published, new items available in stores and, incredibly enough, a whole list of other blog sites offering similar amazing insights. I immediately realised how business-savvy these ladies were. They were using their blogs not only to inspire people, but also to market their products through their businesses. I happened upon a blog written by a lovely lady called Loani Prior, an avid knitter who resided in Noosa. Before long, I realised that she wasn't just some lady from Noosa who liked to knit, but in fact she had just written her second book and was currently touring Australia visiting many of the famous knitting hangouts. She was well respected and well known among wool enthusiasts and here she was, blogging away, without me even knowing about it. I could have met this wonderful lady at her annual events and learnt about new trends within the craft — all via her blog site.

Loani used her blog to not only market her book, but also to engage potential book buyers in discussions about what they'd like to see in her future publications. Just when you think you've learnt everything about the world of business, new technologies give you more ways to connect with more customers and possibly market your business more effectively. I love it!

What is a blog?

Blog is short for 'weblog'. It's usually part of a website maintained by an individual and includes regular commentary, observations, descriptions of events, as well as other material such as graphics, video, or even personal photos and drawings. A blog can also be described as an online diary for business and non-business owners alike. Generally the 'blogger' (the person writing the blog) will use their blog site as an opportunity to discuss their chosen topic and they then may get feedback from those following the site. Many new business owners have their store's website up and running, complete with online blog attached, as a useful tool for creating and maintaining a solid customer base.

A perfect example of the power of a blog is the one written by Jane Brocket, the UK's version of Martha Stewart. Jane started her famous blog site, Yarnstorm, as a means of sharing her life of domesticity with thousands of like-minded women across her country. Before long, Jane's blog site became a world of its own. Her readers stretch across many countries and continents. Jane has published four books purely based on her love of domestic life — no store, no business — just a little blog that grew and grew into so much more.

Blogs can also be a cost-effective way to keep a business advertising and marketing budget to a minimum. Advertising your upcoming special events or sales on your blog will keep your customers coming back for more. Keep in mind that many women love knowing what other women are doing in business and that they enjoy catching up with new trends in the market.

I've spoken of my love for knitting on a few occasions now. It used to be my little 'thing' to do when I had a spare minute or two to relax. My poor knitting has now been badly neglected owing to my obsession with blog searching. One of my favourite things to do if I have a spare half an hour or so is to go blog searching. I love finding out about new techniques and innovations in wool.

Reading blogs is a great way to learn about your craft and your business. In many circumstances, creating your own blog site can be an invaluable way to keep in touch with your existing customer base and potentially an easy way to add new clientele.

It's important when creating a blog site to make sure it's up to date and original. You must love writing, and more importantly you can't be shy about promoting yourself and your business online. If you find it tedious to type a few emails each day, then you probably won't be a diligent and creative blogger. Updating your blog shouldn't be a persistent chore. In fact, you may find it quite uplifting. Considering this marketing option is completely free (other than your time you must devote to it), it may become your most valuable marketing and advertising tool. Nurturing it will only be a positive for the business.

There are hundreds of boring and outdated blogs in cyberspace and they're not doing any justice to their businesses or giving them marketing assistance. An innovative, creative and consistently updated blog will have you drooling for more. Look at any one of my favourite blog sites listed below and you will instantly see what a positive and effective marketing tool blogs can be.

- **www.yarnstorm.blogs.com**
- **www.thepurlbee.com**
- **annamariahorner.blogspot.com**
- **attic24.typepad.com**

How to start your own blog

Do you own a computer that's connected to the internet? Well, you can start your own blog! If you're setting up a website as part of your business, ask your web designer to incorporate a blog section into the site as an easy way to kick things off. Check out other sites that have blogs attached so you know exactly the sort of look you like. Even if you're just in the 'idea' phase of your business, you can still create a blog site through various internet 'how to' sites. Here are a few:

- **www.wikihow.com** A must for all. It's an easy step-by-step guide to starting your first blog as well as anything else you need to know about.
- **www.blogger.com** A free publishing tool from Google.
- **www.howtostartablog.com**
- **www.typepad.com** The premier blogging service for professionals and small businesses. It hosts many popular blogs and small business websites.
- **www.wordpress.com** Another easy-to-use and very popular site.

Don't be scared — you can do it! And the great thing is that you can create your little onsite diary and write whatever you feel about anything. If you're lucky enough, people out there in cyberspace may write to you and give you useful feedback to promote and enhance your business.

Blog your way to extra cash

Most people using the internet for business would have noticed that blogging has become an amazing marketing and advertising tool. Take for example one of my favourite blogs, The Purl Bee. The company has two stores based in New York — one is devoted to knitting (Purl Soho) and the other to sewing (Purl Patchwork). The Purl Bee's blog encompasses both these crafts and is a diarised account of what's happening at the two stores, for example dates for visiting teachers, upcoming events, new trends, etc. Taking it one step further, The Purl Bee's blog now sells advertising space right around the world on their site. Not only are they advertising their own businesses, but they're generating capital by selling advertising space. The other great point is that they are generating capital for their business and not outlaying any extra time or effort to do so. I love it!

Internet advertising

Pay-per-click (PPC) advertising is an internet advertising model used on websites, whereby advertisers pay their website host only when their advertisement is clicked. Advertisers typically bid on keyword phrases relevant to their target market. Content sites commonly charge a fixed price per click rather than use a bidding system. For a great example of this, see the blog for The Purl Bee (www. thepurlbee.com). The site has advertising running down either side of the main text.

Cost-per-click (CPC) advertising refers to money an advertiser pays to a search engine or another internet publisher, with the amount depending on how many single clicks an advertiser gets on its advertisement. One click represents a visitor to its website.

How much are these 'clicks' worth? Well, there are two principal models for determining a cost per click — the flat-rate and the bid-based. In the flat-rate model, the advertiser and publisher agree upon a set amount that will be paid for each click. In both cases the advertiser must consider the potential value of a click from a given source.

In the bid-based model, the advertiser signs a contract that allows them to compete against other advertisers in a private auction hosted by the advertising network. Each advertiser informs the host of the maximum amount that he or she is willing to pay for a given ad spot (often based on a keyword). The auction plays out in an automated fashion every time a visitor triggers the ad spot.

Google AdWords, Yahoo! Search Marketing and Microsoft adCenter are the three largest network operators. All operate under a bid-based model. Cost per click (CPC) varies depending on the search engine and the level of competition for a particular keyword.

What is Twitter and tweeting?

I confess — I don't 'tweet' or do the whole 'Twitter' thing. I'm aware of the concept and the reasoning behind it, but I've never partaken. Since hosting *The Biggest Loser*, I've had many of my blog readers ask me if I'm on Twitter and I feel older than my 36 years when I reply that I don't really have a great understanding of it. I do know that Ashton Kutcher (Demi Moore's husband) has the most 'followers' in the world, with reality star Kim Kardashian following closely behind. These devotees tweet about the happenings in their daily lives, but many small business owners are getting on the Twitter bandwagon to promote events and new stock, among other things. I love buying products from businesses where I know and respect the owner. If the owner of my favourite craft store was on Twitter (you know who you are), I would surely be a follower. Twitter has become an important part of the websites of a few swim schools in Melbourne and Sydney and is now becoming an important technology requirement for various types of businesses.

So what is Twitter and how does it work? Twitter is a social networking and microblogging service that enables its users to send and read messages known as tweets. All users can send and receive tweets via the Twitter website's Short Message Service (SMS). While the service itself costs nothing to use, accessing it through SMS may incur phone service provider fees. The website currently has more than 100 million users worldwide. Many businesses use Twitter as an important marketing tool for updating their customers about products and services. You'll notice that many business websites now have the all-familiar Twitter logo attached to their site.

Do you think you're ready to try Twitter (that's if you're not already using it)? These websites will be useful.

- **www.wikihow.com/Use-Twitter**
- **www.purplecar.net/2009/03/how-to-start-using-twitter/**
- **twitter.zappos.com/start**

Websites

Even though your small business can function perfectly well without a website, your competitors will definitely have a major advantage if they have one and you don't. A hot-looking website, brimming with creativity and jam-packed with information, impresses your customers and can bolster your sales. Think of your website as an opportunity to be as innovative as you want to be. And seriously — are there many businesses nowadays that don't have one?

When I first opened the swim school, my brother Adam (who is a web designer) created a website for me. It was an extremely useful way to promote my new business and let people know I'd opened. Depending on your budget, you can start out small and simple to begin with and then work your way up to large and extravagant when you have a little extra money to outlay. Certainly, if you have an internet-based business that's solely selling goods from a website, you're going to have a very professional-looking and extremely functional site. Hopefully, you can invest quite a few of your budget dollars into creating a fantastic website because you won't have to pay rent for office space or for a 'bricks and mortar' store.

I believe that any type of website is better than none at all. I discontinued my business website a couple of years ago, because I'd been told by Westfield that they were redeveloping the site and my business would be discontinuing within months. I thought it was best to stop promoting the school so that potential customers wouldn't make enquiries and presume I'd still be trading in that location in a year's time. With the benefit of hindsight, I should have continued with the website and maybe posted a little note informing clients that I might be closing. In some ways, it's lucky I didn't — the swim school stayed open for a further three years, even though I'd been told that closure was 'imminent'.

I was also clinging to this silly notion that my main goal was to remain a 'boutique' business. I didn't want to become a powerful business baroness with a multitude of swim schools, so I thought it was a waste to spend heaps of money on marketing and advertising on the internet. Oh, how business-unsavvy I was! If I'd known what I know now, I would have kept my website running and I'd be blogging away and getting feedback from my customers. We live and learn!

That said, my advice to you all is to create a website! You'll realise the power that it brings, even if you're not a blogger, tweeter or Facebooker. Keep in mind that a website is sometimes the first thing people see when they become acquainted with your business. For instance, I happened upon a brand-new yarn store in Brisbane when I was flipping through a magazine. I thought it would make sense to check out their website first before making the trek to the other side of the city. As soon as the homepage popped up on my computer screen, I was completely blown away. If my boys hadn't needed to be picked up from school, I would have been there in a flash. Viewing the website had immediately given a great impression and I really wanted to check this place out. First impressions do last, so make your website something to remember.

Creating your own website

There are three main steps to creating your own website:

1. Get a domain name;

2. Plan and design it; and

3. Find a host

In basic terms, a domain name is your address on the web. It's the sequence of words and letters that customers type into their browser to find you on the internet, for example:

www._____

Your domain name will be divided up into distinct sections, with each section separated by a full stop:

- **www.** — World Wide Web
- **yarnstorm.** — name of establishment or entity
- **com.** — type of organisation
- **au** — country code

A domain name can be a combination of letters and numbers of up to 63 characters. Don't go crazy with the whole '63' option, though! It's probably wise to keep your name as catchy and as simple as possible. The characters authorised in your domain name are those from A to Z, the numbers from zero to nine and hyphens may also be used. Domain names cannot begin or end with a hyphen or have two hyphens in a row. No other characters are allowed, for example &, *, ! , %.

Learn the lingo

I never really knew why some websites had .com and others were .com.au or .net.au. If you're in the same boat, this list (kindly provided by my brother) will fill you in. It may help you choose an appropriate domain name.

- .com — used and recognised worldwide and is available to any individual, business or organisation
- .com.au — commercial entities in Australia
- .net — the fourth most popular top-level domain, used by any individual, business or organisation. Generally used for technology-based businesses or companies
- .net.au — commonly commercial entities and technology-based companies or businesses in Australia
- .org — initially used for non-profit organisations but now is the third most widely used domain. Although .org was recommended for non-commercial entities, there are no restrictions to registration. There are many instances of .org being used by commercial sites
- .org.au — associations and non-profit organisations (i.e., non-commercial organisations) in Australia
- .edu.au — Australian educational institutions
- .gov.au — Australian governments and their departments
- .id.au — for Australian residents or citizens; cannot be used for any commercial services
- .asn.au — associations and non-profit organisations in Australia
- .info — derived from the word 'information', indicating that the domain is intended for informative internet resources; unrestricted and available to everyone
- .biz — intended to be used by businesses; anyone doing business via the internet is authorised to use it

Make sure your domain name is coherent and not just a jumble of words. It would be a crying shame if your website was fabulous but no one could remember the name because it was so obscure! Don't choose a random or irrelevant name either, or one that doesn't reflect the nature of your business. If you're opening a store-based business then most likely your website name will be the same name as your business, but there may be certain circumstances where you require something different. If this is the case, it comes down to choosing something that will work best for your business's longevity and branding.

There are many places where you can register your domain name, including www.domainregistration.com.au and www.crazydomains.com.au

Design it yourself

If money is tight and you feel you have the flair, finesse and know-how to create your own site, these places may help get you on the right track:

- **www.4creatingawebsite.com** This free and fantastic site will walk you through each step for designing and posting your website.
- **www.flyingsolo.com.au** An easy and simple-to-use program to guide you through setting up a website on your own.

Do your research

Let's face it — we all love the internet. It's a vast treasure trove of information where you can find out just about anything on everything! Make a note of the websites you really love and analyse those that don't appeal. Ask yourself why some things work and others don't. Take bits and pieces of inspiration from various sites and try to construct one that incorporates all your favourite things. Remember, the sky's the limit. You are only limited by your imagination and creativity. Don't be concerned about having a similar layout to other businesses — customise your site with different colours, fonts and pictures.

Build baby build

Now it's time to get building. The majority of small businesses commission a website designer to create and then construct a website. You can do it yourself for free, but make sure you consider how important the website will be to your business. Are you confident you can create something really professional and totally impressive? Remember: the first place your competition and your clientele might look if they're doing some background research is — that's right — your website.

Constructing your website is a bit like renovating your home — there are lots of dodgy shysters out there ready to take you for a ride and empty your wallet. As with all professions, web designers can range quite broadly in terms of credibility and experience. Like your home renovations, get three or more quotes and then ask to see examples of their handiwork. A designer's company logo or name often appears at the bottom of a website. Choose the layouts you like and then contact the designer for a quote.

The layout of your website is crucial to its effectiveness. There's nothing worse than looking up a website and then being completely confused by the information on the screen. A potential customer's needs are simple: they want a concise, engaging and user-friendly site that's easy to navigate. Try to avoid clutter and confusion with information overload. An overly busy website may project the image of a disorganised business that won't be able to deliver products or services promptly or efficiently. Keep your homepage catchy and users will want to delve further into the site. It's really important to help them do this by making the site easy to navigate. Try to get the balance between the 'wow' factor and simple elegance.

Top tips for website success

If you're ready to join the World Wide Web of advertising, and possibly add greatly to your customer base, follow these great tips for creating a truly stand-out site:

- Write down the major headings you'll need for a useful, workable and informative website. For example, if you're a wedding or event coordinator, your might have:
  — About us
  — Testimonials
  — Our services
  — Online shop (can be added later to the original website)
  — Contact us
  — Blog

Under these headings, write all the information that the customer will require, for example street address, email, and contact phone numbers under Contact Us. Keep it simple. Internet users (including me) find it really frustrating to visit a website and get completely lost because there are too many tabs to press.

- Visit your website designer armed with all your information. During this design and construction phase, you can always add or delete any information that's not relevant to your business.
- Considering your advertising budget may not be stacked full of money, think about other places where you may be able to promote your website once it's up and running, for example:
  - Include your details on receipts or dockets. People often keep receipts for warranty or returns purposes and may notice that you're available online.
  - Spruik your website address to journalists or columnists that may be writing an advertorial or newspaper article when your business first starts trading.
  - Ask (nicely) to be included on the blogs of friends or business associates. (Don't you just love it when friends have blogs with hundreds of followers?) I know it's a tad cheeky, but more often than not a friend is happy to help out. It only takes one person to love your website and it may catch on like wildfire.

My little tips

- Beware of the paraphernalia from marketing and advertising companies — chose wisely before you outlay a lot of money.
- Do your research again — find out where your customers are and target those areas.
- Be innovative! You don't have to spend a lot of money.
- Be open to using a professional — it may cost you more but could be more effective in some instances.
- Try to keep up to date with new technology — social networking and the internet are fast becoming *the* marketing and publicity tools.

Location, Location

Storefront businesses

If you're a big fan of the TV series *Seinfeld*, then you'll be familiar with the episode where Jerry talks about the shops near his apartment and how they appear to be the 'revolving shops'. One day there's a dry cleaner occupying the space, and before you can blink there's an Indian restaurant in its place.

This seems to happen in all neighbourhoods. If you're anything like me, you find yourself hoping that the new tenant finally finds success in that 'cursed' location where others have failed. Regrettably, many businesses close down after a seemingly short time and it makes me wonder what was behind their demise. In some cases the location was fantastic, signage and marketing were professional and, most significantly, there were no other direct competitors trading in the general vicinity. Where did things go wrong?

I think women have wonderfully intuitive instincts about things in general, which provides us with an advantage over our male counterparts when it comes to choosing the right location for just about everything — better spots at the beach, more comfortable location for a picnic, more accessible parking positions, and the lists goes on. (I'm sure my husband, brother and dad would have a different opinion about this.) Many of us love to shop and often have an uncanny knack (I call it an 'inner shopping compass') that helps us gravitate towards certain fabulous precincts. There are exceptions, of course, and having the best location isn't always the key to success. Take my favourite fabric store, for example. It's not located in a major shopping centre, it has no other stores around it of interest to me, it's located in a run-down industrial park *and* it's on the other side of the city. So, why do I go there if the location is undesirable? Why is it always packed with cheery customers forking out loads of money? Answer: the service is great, their product is exceptional, no other business in Brisbane stocks their fabric and they are up to date with current fads and trends. All that being said, they had already built up a loyal customer base over 10 years in the former location (a shopping centre) and that has held them in good stead. It would be interesting to see if a brand-new small business could survive in the same location if they were just starting out.

In most situations, a great position is the key. I was talking to a girlfriend recently about my ultimate business (yes, a yarn store. I may be obsessed!) and I found myself telling her that even if I wasn't flat out with the swim school, my two boys and *The Biggest Loser*, I still wouldn't open up a yarn store simply because there's nothing desirable for lease — at least not in close vicinity to my house and away from my competitors.

I only recently visited my favourite yarn store on the north side of Brisbane and got talking with one of the store's wonderful owners. She had recently moved from another location about 20 minutes further north and had been worried that her customers may not travel to the new location. Needless to say, she didn't have any reason to be concerned. One week after opening I decided to check out the new store and it was absolutely pumping! The customers were queuing out the door and, being the entrepreneur that she is, she'd opened up an amazing coffee shop next door. She was knee-deep in boxes with new stock just delivered, there was a table full of ladies that had just arrived to do a cable-knit class and a booth starting the next day at the annual craft fair.

'How's everything going?' I asked tentatively.

'Well, I feel like I should be absolutely exhausted and overwhelmed by everything I have to do, so I guess I must be running on adrenalin because I feel full of energy and excitement rather than being worried. I don't know why I thought having to re-locate my business could possibly be my downfall! To be honest, there probably needs to be at least 30 hours in the day instead of 24, but things will get done — they always do,' she confessed.

This woman was living my dream!

This is a great example of how a location change doesn't necessarily spell disaster for a business. In this case, the owner kept her existing clientele, and then enhanced their experience with the addition of a coffee shop. The change of location didn't affect her bottom line, her financial strength or her customer loyalty.

Finding out that you have to vacate a leased store can be a daunting prospect also, but if your products and services are worth it, your clientele are sure to follow, especially if you make the new store even more amazing than the last. Give customers a reason to want to stick with you — and they most probably will.

My location

I chose a major shopping centre as the location to build my swim school because I had only one option in mind and I was stubbornly sticking to it. I was so adamant that my actual business would replicate my dream business that nothing else had a chance to figure in the equation. Big mistake! I often wonder where we'd be now if we'd chosen somewhere else. I realise now that I should have considered other locations or options for my swim school instead of having such tunnel vision on the shopping centre location.

My other main hurdle was that we were trailblazers in having a swim school located in a shopping centre and this meant that researching the idea or even going on a reconnaissance mission to 'suss out' the opposition was impossible in those vital planning stages. Don't get me wrong — the opportunity to have the amount of walk-by traffic means limited advertising is required. There's also the added attraction and convenience of being located in one of Australia's largest shopping centres. My clientele seem to enjoy the opportunity to combine swimming lessons for the kids with a coffee or the weekly food-shopping trip, but there are many, many overheads for me as an owner, of course. Would I do things differently if I had my time over? Probably not, because I feel like I've got something special happening and my clients obviously think so too.

Westfield had originally offered me a second-floor space, which had a good vibe, but not a great vibe. My female instincts must have been well and truly working overtime because something inside me was telling me that the position just wasn't 'it'. I was excited nevertheless that I'd even been offered the opportunity so I wasn't about to start getting choosy. After many exciting visits to the proposed location, I talked myself into how I could make it work even though it was quite small and tucked away in the corner. The gods of small business must have been looking down on me because a couple of weeks later I was advised that the location wasn't structurally sound to hold a swimming pool and they had another location for me to look at.

I wondered if this was a bad omen. The site they'd suggested wasn't really familiar to me. I'd visited the centre a few times a week, every week, over the years, so should I really be considering a location that I couldn't even visualise? Would people venture down that end of the building? If I was challenged at this stage of the proceedings, was I indeed cut out to run my own business at all?

I remember getting off the phone from the centre's leasing manager and immediately ringing my husband at work to tell him the latest machinations.

'Well, let's not think anything too negative until we actually see,' he said, with less enthusiasm than I had hoped.

'No, I have to go right now. Can you meet me on your way home from work?' I pleaded, with almost too much impatience in my tone. 'I can't wait that long!'

'Um, do I have a choice?' he asked, knowing the answer all too well.

I literally could not wait an extra day to see the site, and I certainly wouldn't be able to sleep that night without being able to consider the new location. I bundled my four-year-old into the car and made the 10-minute drive to the proposed location. When we arrived, I told Jacob to go around the corner and look straight ahead at the centre's child-care centre and tell me whether he thought it was a good spot for Mummy to build a pool. He walked around the corner and within five seconds, he popped his head back around and said, 'Perfect spot, Mummy!'

I hugged him and continued around the corner. I closed my eyes and stood right in front of the tenancy. After a few long seconds I managed to find the courage to open my eyes. I knew instantly that it was the ideal spot for my swimming school! It had a certain presence about it that gave a completely positive feeling. It was also located next door to the council library — what a bonus.

'Is it a good spot, Mummy?' Jacob asked.

'It's a great spot!' I replied, with excitement.

And that was that — the Hayley Lewis Swim School was born, and my life would never be the same again.

The reconnaissance mission

Wouldn't it be fantastic if we could all own our dream business just down the road from where we live and where our children attend school. Travelling time would be cut to a minimum and it would generally make life a lot easier. Unfortunately, this isn't possible for everyone, so you need to find the best possible location for the business and your own personal circumstances.

It's vital that you spend a great deal of time looking for a 'home' for your business. Where would you and your girlfriends like to shop? What will draw customers to your location? Do other businesses draw customers to the area? Take the time to scope out the competition. Search for shops for lease and do your homework by contacting real estate agents about lease terms and rental fees. Generally, you should get an instant feel for the location when you find it. Make sure it ticks all the boxes before even considering it. Here are few things to consider:

- **Similar businesses in the area** Try to find a location that isn't saturated with similar businesses to your own. Look instead for an area or precinct that has complementary businesses. An area with bustling coffee shops and trendy clothing stores would be suitable for a bookstore or craft outlet because like-minded people are already browsing in the vicinity.

- **Travel time from home, schools and family help** Location doesn't matter to some people. For mothers, however, the location of their business is crucial to the day-to-day running of the family. My good friends own a boutique and during the course of a week they spend more than 12 hours in the car driving to and from work. In a small city like Brisbane, this is quite remarkable. Personally, I couldn't do it. My swim school is located about 11 minutes from my front door and some days it seems like it takes a lifetime to get home. You need to weigh up your family's needs as well as what you think you are capable of achieving. On those stressful days, when nothing goes to plan, you might be truly grateful that you don't have an hour's commute home.

- **Previous businesses** Ask the landlord who occupied the space before you and the nature of their business. It may be worth finding out how long each tenant rented the property and possibly the reasons behind why they left (although the landlord may not want to divulge this information). Have a poke around and ask other business owners to fill you in on the details. Chances are you already know the type of business that was carried out. If this is the case, ask yourself, 'Would I stop here to shop?'

- **Convenience of location** The world seems to be getting faster and we are all getting busier, so convenience is a big factor when it comes to any type of shopping. Try to find a location that's convenient. It doesn't have to be a major shopping centre, which caters for convenience but also charges high rent for the privilege. Look for a great position that people already frequent. I often pass little stores that look great and I'm tempted to stop and check them out, but more often than not I don't. The reason is simple: I don't really want to stop for just one store. I know it sounds crazy, but if there was at least one other interesting shop, then that would encourage my curiosity and strengthen my reason to take a look inside.

- **Good parking facilities** I have this absolutely amazing boutique close to where I live, but the parking is horrendous. The traffic in the area is manic and I feel stressed just thinking about driving there. Parking spaces are limited and if you miss out, the closest parking is half a kilometre away. Don't get me wrong — I love to walk. In fact, I power-walk every day. But that doesn't mean I want to sweat it out with an armful of shopping bags in the summer heat. Assess your potential area. Many locations offer specific parking for your customers, as well as having off-street parking close by. Before you sign any rental agreements, make sure you've fully considered the parking factor, because a certain type of clientele won't venture out unless they can park within a stone's throw of the store.

- **Close to public transport** Your business may cater to people of all ages and demographics. Many potential customers won't have their own transport, so it's important you are located close to public transport routes.

- **Desirable area and storefront** You can't always start out in the prettiest or wealthiest areas, but that doesn't mean that you can't create a gorgeous and enticing storefront for your customers. Look at the surrounding stores (if you are in a shopping precinct) and decide whether you'd like to have them as neighbours. Do they take pride in their shopfront and window displays? Do the premises look clean and tidy, inside and out? If you can't answer yes to both questions, then appearance could become a bugbear when you start your business. My swim school sits beside the local library. Fortunately, they have cleaners caring for the upkeep of the premises on a daily basis — they're perfect neighbours. Not far from me, however, is a coffee shop and smokers often stand outside my premises and drop their cigarette butts on the ground — great neighbours, but thoughtless customers.

  Locate your business close to other like-minded and 'proud' small business owners. This will reduce your level of frustration with less-than-fussy neighbours immensely.

- **Cost of rent and lease terms and conditions** A huge chunk of your monthly expenses goes towards rent, so you must factor this into your business budget. You may be one of the lucky ones that has either great cash flow or a rich aunty who can bail you out if the chips are down. More likely, you're one of the greater percentage of people that is doing it the tough way by taking out a bank loan or investing your life savings into your business. If so, investigate the leasing arrangements thoroughly and make sure you are comfortable with your location's rental fee. Take time to read through the terms of your lease and then obtain advice from a solicitor. This is money well spent, believe me. It may be the last place you want to spend your hard-earned cash, but you cannot possibly put a price on peace of mind.

Location questionnaire

Location choice can make or break a small business. Put your possible location to the test by answering the following important questions:

1. Have you already sourced potential locations?

2. If yes, have you investigated rental or leasing costs?

3. Is it important to be near your home base?

4. How far, or for how long, would you be prepared to travel each day to and from your business?

5. Are there similar businesses within a 1-kilometre radius of your proposed location? If so, how many?

6. Do you have more than one location in mind? If so, list the pros and cons of each location.

7. Is your rent on par with other businesses in the area of the same size?

Make it a priority to choose a location that gives you a positive vibe. Don't settle for second best. If your dream location is too pricey or too far to travel, then keep looking. This is a super-important part of your business plan and a major factor in the success of your business, so don't skimp on research or jump into an agreement you'll regret later. It's worth holding back your business start-up date in order to find something that not only fits your budget but also excites and inspires you.

A home-based business

Many small business owners start off in home-based set-ups. Some gradually move on to outside premises as the business begins to expand, and in other cases, a storefront isn't needed to run the business successfully, so home remains the perfect place. Obviously, if your business is internet-based and you are a sole operator with no employees, then home may be ideal.

With the colossal growth and speed of technology and technology-based business, the number of home offices in Australia has increased considerably. Technological breakthroughs have made it easier to conduct our businesses on the run, in our cars and indeed, at home. I was watching *Oprah* (as you do, when you work from home!) and Sir Richard Branson, the founder of the Virgin Group, was giving a tour of his island paradise. I found it very enlightening to hear that he hadn't spent many days working from his actual place of business, preferring to conduct his day-to-day business in the peace and quiet of his home. Wouldn't it be nice if the secret to business success was never actually going to the office!

Things are obviously catching on here in Australia because according to the Australian Bureau of Statistics, 21 per cent of businesses operate from home. In fact, it estimates that there are more than 850,000 home-based businesses. There are many pros and cons in the working-from-home debate. If you are seriously considering this as an option, you may like to consider the following advantages:

Advantages
- No storefront rental or leasing costs.
- No costs involved in travelling to and from the workplace.
- No travel time.
- No dress code — you can work all day in your pyjamas.
- No distinct office hours in some circumstances.

Although there are many advantages to a home-based business, there are also certain disadvantages. I've never owned or operated a home business, but a huge part of my workload managing the swim school is done at home. Unfortunately, I find there is sometimes a stigma attached to the working-from-home scenario. I can see the smirk on a person's face when I say, 'I can't have a coffee today — I'm working from home.' Then comes the curious little smile that makes me feel like I'm telling a lie. I feel that I have to justify myself or explain the actual jobs I'll be doing, just to prove that I am, in fact, working!

Working from home requires a certain kind of dedication. It took me a little time to adjust when I started writing this book. My family and I didn't realise straightaway that my little room had instantly become my workplace. I didn't decide to write because I was bored or needed something to do in my spare time. It's something I've always wanted to do, but with it came responsibilities and deadlines. While I still managed and owned the swim school, I had to dedicate a certain amount of hours per day to writing or I simply knew I wouldn't finish it. Goodbye writing career.

Don't get me wrong; I've loved the writing process. It's given me an even greater respect for writers of all genres. But to complete a manuscript for a book, you have to approach it like any job. Like many home businesses, my sewing-cum-ironing room was transformed into a home office. Yes, small tears were shed in the process, as my beloved knitting needles, wool, sewing machine and fabrics were put into cupboards to make way for a laptop, whiteboard, stationery and all things business. My road bike was replaced with a gigantic calendar on my whiteboard with my set word counts and deadline dates.

Another important aspect of your home business education is that distraction can be your biggest enemy. It took me a good couple of months to shut myself off from doing household chores sporadically throughout the day. I would tend to write for 30 minutes, put on a load of washing or do the vacuuming, return to my desk for another 30 minutes and then continue to follow this ridiculous regime right throughout the day until 2.30 p.m. when it was school pick-up time. I would subsequently lose my train of thought as soon as I got up from the computer. Both the housework and my writing became a jumbled and chaotic mess, which became both frustrating and tiring. I realised when my word count was suffering that my time-management skills needed a massive overhaul. Housework needed to be one entity and writing needed to be another, both requiring their very own allotted time and focus.

Another important 'distraction buster' is to make sure others understand that just because you're at home working doesn't mean that you're available for a 'quick chat' or a 'quick cuppa'. My husband runs his physiotherapy business from home on Fridays. I didn't really respect that these days were working days for him, and I always saw it as his opportunity to have a day off. Having Fridays at home together because we were both working, it didn't take him long to realise that 'door shut' meant that serious work was taking place inside. It was difficult but essential for getting the job done.

Don't get me wrong, taking regular breaks is important, especially if you are working on a computer all day. Just make sure they're not 'random' breaks. Make set times during the day for a minimum of three breaks — one mini-break mid morning, a longer break at lunchtime and another mini-break mid afternoon. Time away from the computer to rest your eyes and to have a good stretch is key to a successful home–work routine.

I must admit, working from home does have some lovely perks. I do love being in my cosy room with the heater on, puppy dog Daisy at my feet on a warm rug and my cup of coffee sitting beside me. Serious work is being done, I promise!

As with everything, you do have to weigh up what is best for your business and your current situation. If you know that having a storefront is crucial to your business but you haven't got the cash flow available to cover the rental costs, then maybe you need to consider waiting until you are in a healthier financial position.

Disadvantages
- Distractions from family members or housemates.
- Distractions of housework, television and anything else that may be more interesting than actual work itself.
- Without a visual place of business in terms of a bricks and mortar store, your advertising and marketing budget may need to be significantly larger in order to let your potential customers know about your business and what products or services you are providing.
- Not being able to get into the 'zone' to do work because you haven't left your home.
- A home-based business without employees may become a major issue if you need to be surrounded by people to remain 'sane and upbeat'.
- You may find yourself always in your office doing work because it's easily accessible. This may cause problems with family members.

Planning your home office
This can be more challenging than you might think, especially if you don't have adequate space in which to fit the components of your business. Let's presume you have some space, be it small or substantial, otherwise you wouldn't be considering working from home. To run a successful and

organised home business you need to be able to cope with a wide variety of issues, so it will be extremely important to take the time to research and plan exactly what you require from the home office.

Obviously, a home-based office should be functional and it should model a real working environment for you and your employees (if you have any). The layout will depend on your living arrangements, for example whether you have a partner and small children or if you share with a housemate.

This isn't the time to slap a few filing cabinets together in the vain hope of managing and developing your business empire. Here are a few questions to consider:

- **Will your equipment fit the available space?** Write down the necessary equipment and your furniture requirements. Obviously, your desk and storage systems will be vital to the layout. If your finances allow it, spend the maximum amount possible on a functional and accommodating desk. This doesn't mean you need to cover every square centimetre with clutter either — desk clutter can lead to 'mind clutter' and this may set you on the path to disarray and disorganisation. If you're the only person occupying the space, think about the accessibility of the equipment in the space, for example, if you know that you use your fax machine frequently, place it close by for easy access. Don't pop it on a top shelf so it's difficult to send and receive your fax messages. Have your phone centrally located and not somewhere that requires you to get up and down constantly.

- **Do you have enough cupboard or shelf space for stock?** There are many companies nowadays that specialise in spectacular storage solutions. It's possible to transform the pokiest workspace or tiniest office into a functional and organised storage and distribution centre with the proper shelving system.

- **Can the space accommodate other staff?** Your workspace may need to be separate to that of your employees. In certain circumstances, it may be wise to work in an area that is disconnected from your staff so that you can conduct business privately. At the swim school, our main desk is located front and centre, so I'm grateful for a bit of privacy if I need to make phone calls that aren't relevant to the staff. Sometimes you just need a separate space for contemplation too, especially if your business relies on creativity and innovation.

- **If you have employees, can they work in close proximity to one another?** Two staff members may require twin work areas but can easily share filing and cupboard space. If your business is predominantly conducted on the phone, make sure you have enough privacy and space to be able to talk to clients without hearing other employees' conversations.

- **Will the home business cope with growth?** This is something to seriously consider. When it happens (and let's hope it does!), be prepared for the possibility that you'll need a bigger space — or simply a bigger home. Also remember that with growth comes an increasing amount of paperwork. Make sure your storage space is well prepared for loads of paper or large computer storage facilities. Filing cabinets are without doubt my favourite asset in both my home office and my swim school office. I have sturdy magazine holders for periodicals and big binders for all my statements. I must admit that I love stationery, so I'll buy anything that is new and exciting on the market in a flash.

- **Will you be holding meetings at home?** If so, have you got an area that's suitable for conducting formal discussions with potential clients or customers? Projecting a professional, well-organised and structured image is paramount to a home-based business. First impressions last and you don't want a potential customer or client meeting you in a workspace that looks like a bomb hit it. Try to create a stylish, comfortable and functional area. It should have a relaxed atmosphere that spells 'success' and shows that you have pride in your workspace and in the product or service you're selling. Keep things simple: clean, white walls, comfortable chairs/sofa, a few stylish prints and some nice candles will go a long way to impressing people.

There's a wide range of government obligations that may apply to operating a small business from home, including: taxation, employment, council approval and licensing. Make sure you're aware of anything that may affect you.

Your legal obligations

The Australian Taxation Office (ATO) requires you to declare all sources of income and have evidence of all your deductions for expenditure incurred while operating the business. You need to keep the following records for five years after they are prepared, obtained, or the transaction is completed:

- receipts for supplies, acquisitions and other expenses
- wages records

You may need to register or apply to the ATO for some or all of the following:

- Tax file number (TFN)
- Australian business number (ABN)
- Goods and services tax (GST)
- Pay as you go (PAYG)
- Fringe benefits tax (FBT)
- Capital gains tax (CGT) — important if you are claiming some of your home costs as a tax deduction
- Superannuation guarantee charge (SGC)

Some other important considerations are:
- **Can you conduct the type of business you want under local council regulations?**
- **What are the town planning requirements of your local government authority?**

Legal requirements for employees
Whether it be a storefront business or a home-based one, you want to make sure you are hiring the right people for the job. Just because you run your business from your home, it doesn't

mean that your legal obligations are waived in relation to your employees. You also have obligations under federal, state and territory laws; industrial awards and agreements; tribunal decisions; and contracts of employment — written or verbal.

Some of those obligations are:

- paying correct wages
- reimbursing your employees for work-related expenses
- ensuring a safe working environment for you and your staff.

These are just a few obligations that you must adhere to as a home-based employer. Even if you are employing friends and family members, you need to follow the appropriate path otherwise legal issues may arise.

It's vital to do your research. Here are some important and useful websites to check out before starting a home-based business:

- **www.business.gov.au** I've mentioned this site on a few occasions, but it really is a gem. Did you know that as a home-based business owner you are eligible to receive a grant or assistance from the government? It's a wonderful incentive for budding entrepreneurs reluctant to start a business because of financial constraints. This excellent website covers loads of issues, including: licences and registrations; employing people; taxation; importing and exporting; and fair trading. You must remember to cover all bases and this website makes sure you've considered all angles. Make sure you stay on top of any changes that may occur from time to time in relation to the structure and set-up of your home-based business.

- **www.centrelink.gov.au** Centrelink may contact you from time to time if you have any employees receiving payments through them as well as being employed by you. Make sure you are maintaining the right paperwork for these employees or contact Centrelink if you have any questions.

Case study: **Tracey Taylor & Dee Green**

I've been very fortunate over the past 20 years to have two amazingly inspirational and talented women in my life. They are godmothers to my sons and never cease to amaze me with their relentless need for fun and adventure, as well as their insatiable appetite for business. They truly represent the quintessential female entrepreneurs in every way. Here is their story:

TRACEY TAYLOR AND DEE GREEN

OFF THE PLANET & 37 FRAMES PHOTOGRAPHY

Running our own business was simply a natural evolution of an unintentional life plan. With hindsight, there was never going to be another realistic option for us. We were destined to be business owners, embracing success and failure, wrong turns, opportunities and challenges. As Henry David Thoreau said: 'Go confidently in the direction of our dreams! Live the life you've imagined.' Taking the road less travelled in a cultural minefield meant ultimately that we both arrived at a home-based business. Twelve years on and living in Tokyo, we are still going strong and are definitely gaining momentum.

Starting our small business was a necessity. The cruel reality was that we needed to eat and to pay rent for our tiny Tokyo shoebox called home. With overheads and rents being astronomical in a retail-cum-lease setting, the only business model that was financially possible was a 'SOHO' (small office/home office). We started our little 'neighbourhood' English school called Off the Planet from our minuscule Tokyo apartment back in 1998. It soon became quite clear that this was a savvy business move. The benefits were obvious: low overheads, shared utilities and rent and no commuting concerns.

Our biggest fear was the potential issues that may emerge when running a bustling business in a neighbourhood environment. We've managed to avoid any major problems throughout the past 12 years by maintaining good relations, politeness and respecting our neighbour's limits and boundaries. From a marketing perspective, we've been successful largely owing to word of mouth, developing sustainable and lasting relationships and living up to expectations and promises. These things have definitely been the biggest business lessons that we've learnt in Japan. When we started, an 'online presence' and blogging weren't relevant or understood, which meant the success of our business hinged on a great product and an impeccable reputation. Of course, we have a basic website now, but generally our business is generated from referrals and introductions to this very day.

The pros generally outweigh the cons when it comes to the daily running of things, but it can be very hard at times to just *leave work*, especially when there's always work to be done and it's just sitting in the next room. The business may be in another area of the apartment, but it is always there, and it's *our* business and *our* heart and soul. There's a lot invested right under our feet, literally.

You may discover, as we both have, that there's always something to be done, like paperwork, cleaning, sorting and further business planning — the list goes on and on. The success of our business partnership comes down to effective prioritising and time management, as well as allowing ourselves a healthy life balance. It's an ongoing work-in-progress that over time finds its own equilibrium.

When starting a home-based business, you need to be extremely focused and you can never, ever give up. You must be willing to change and adapt when the need arises and be open to adopting the mind-set that there is always a way, no matter what the barrier. A critical aspect of success is the all-important planning phase. Initially, we both ignored the actual business practicalities and constructive preparation stage, tending to focus on the creative side. Our advice would be to get into a smooth and realistic system right from the start, for example, creating a system where paperwork is finished each day. You'll soon realise that a good routine will ultimately lead to less work piling up over time, which in turn gives more time for pursuits away from the business. Remember to keep the systems simple and be thoroughly organised with every aspect of the business. If you begin with a great routine, things can only get easier and more manageable as you progress. It will be much more pleasant in the long run if you spend a little extra time working on getting things right from the outset.

Staff

Your business is only as successful as the people directly involved in it. It would be rare if any of your staff worked as hard as you do — after all, it's your business and you have a lot more invested in its success than they do. We soon realised that staffing issues became a problem for us. We experimented with a small staff base at the beginning, but quickly realised that our clientele were only attending the school because of us. We were flattered, naturally, that they wanted our expertise, but we'd hired staff to take some of the pressure off us, but this wasn't meeting client expectations. To this very day, it's still a dilemma. Over time, however, we've found the need to let go a little and to actively search for the right people until we're confident we've got it right.

We still manage the bulk of the school's operating requirements, but we have become quite aware that we couldn't do it without the help of some amazing staff. The best advice that we can give in relation to staffing is don't hire the first person that walks through the door for an interview. They must have the right qualifications and personality for the job, otherwise you're back at square one.

Have a passion or hobby

For as long as we can remember, our passion has been to travel. Fortunately, this passion melded nicely with another — photography. Running our business has meant lots of travel, which evolved into a deep love of photographing the world. This passion has led to two further home-based businesses during our time in Japan: an online scrapbooking store called Scrap the Planet; and our current successful venture, 37 Frames Photography.

Off the Planet was moving along so well and we were in such a good routine that we felt we had time to take on something new. We knew our strength was our creativity, and along with our computer and photography skills we decided to start Scrap the Planet, and it literally took off overnight. When we owned the business there were many days we couldn't get away from the apartment because of the volume of orders. Eventually, we realised that while it was great, we were working non-stop and we regrettably had absolutely no work–life balance whatsoever. The business consumed our entire week, so we made the very difficult decision to move on after three very happy yet exhausting years. We credit the success of Scrap the Planet to a few things: a secure and easy-to-use website, friendly customer service, a regularly updated blog, mini-newsletters and excellent word of mouth. It was extremely hard to let go but now we find ourselves working on our photography in a professional capacity.

With the ongoing success of our English school and the closure of Scrap the Planet, we found ourselves tapping into our entrepreneurial instincts once again. We'd discovered that our strength as small business operators was in service-based business rather than in product-driven ones. Our love of photography has blossomed into a new venture, 37 Frames Photography, which showcases stunning landscapes and life's special moments.

37 Frames Photography is still modelled on our business spirit — a great product that meets and surpasses our clients' expectations. It's a very competitive market, so carving a niche is vital to longevity within the industry. We've realised that our branding and continuity is important, along with the added responsibility of all the

online marketing. The website is important and it enables our clients to view and experience the quality of our work, but it's now the blog and social media interaction that moves faster and has more current content available.

The blog needs constant updates because we've found that it keeps our potential and long-term customers interested in what we are doing next. Facebook and Twitter have also been a great way for us to generate more clients and our monthly online newsletter enables us to promote the business without any costly advertising fees. Technology moves fast these days, so it's important to keep up to date with advances.

Our most crucial piece of advice to all potential home-based business owners is to make an effort to be in the loop and stay there. You'll become more connected and aware of your industry and its future direction. Make sure you spend more time crafting your business rather than worrying about what others are doing. You can, without question, distinguish yourself from your competitors if you create your own signature product or style. Always try to specialise and be open to learning. It goes without saying, but *loving* what you do sets you on the path to greatness, and the personal satisfaction it brings is priceless. We couldn't be more content and are thrilled to be doing what we adore. We are working for ourselves and setting our own goals and this seems to propel us forward and beyond. And we didn't need to leave our house to achieve it!

'Our greatest weakness lies in giving up.
The most certain way to succeed is
always to try just one more time.'

Thomas Edison

My little tips

- Go with your instinct. If the location doesn't feel right, then it probably isn't. Continue to search until it feels right.
- Make sure your location is a good fit for your business venture — a young women's fashion boutique may not do so well in an area where the demographic is older.
- Ideally, your business should not sit in an area that is saturated with like businesses.
- Make sure your location is convenient and accessible to you as well as your customers.
- Home-based businesses should be set up like a professional business with set working times.
- Organise your schedule so that work and home/family life are kept separate.
- Make sure you maintain all your legal obligations.

Markets and Fairs

'Market day' could be 'pay day'!

If you have been reading this book chapter by chapter, you will remember well my own little market business that failed miserably. I can still look back at that experience and see a few positive lessons among the many negative ones. Many entrepreneurs, both here in Australia and overseas, start out in business selling at the markets. I've seen firsthand the success that a young, innovative market-seller can have in my lovely friend Natalie Green. She had been a flight attendant for many years and would often spend her Saturdays at the local markets selling her range of Tickled Pink Cards and various other handmade items. Nat worked every minute she could find (when she wasn't flying the skies) to manufacture her range in her Brisbane apartment in order to start selling at one of Queensland's amazing farmers' markets. Soon after her first stall opening, she relinquished her day job and started focusing on expanding her business across Australia. Even though she now sells to many stores, Nat still spends her Saturdays at the markets, where she has somewhat of a cult following. See her amazing range at www.tickledpinkcards.com.au.

Personally, I love to go to the markets. We're extremely lucky in Australia to have many wonderful markets and local fairs to visit and also have the opportunity to buy fantastic handmade products. It's a good idea to test your product at a market before you start mass-producing or developing it further. You obviously need to do your homework on your competitors, who may be selling similar products at market. It's difficult to sell goods at a market that is already saturated with a particular product. Walk around the various markets in your capital city or large regional town. Many have a different atmosphere or 'feel' when you compare them. Farmers' markets generally concentrate on homegrown produce and homemade goods, while others typically sell goods from overseas. The last thing you want for your potential business and confidence is to try and sell your products in an environment that doesn't have the right buyers. Your product should be a close match with the market's customer base.

If you are thinking about giving your products a test-drive at the markets, *Australian Markets and Fairs* magazine is a great place to do some research. It's published every two months and covers the national market and event circuit. It has every single bit of useful information you will need when starting out. It also offers a comprehensive list of every market and fair within each state in Australia and how often they are run. For more details, you can contact the editor at editor@marketsandfairs.com.au.

Before you start your foray into market trading, you'll need to consider the following:

- **Insurance and Public Liability Cover** There are many different insurance companies that offer fantastic cover for stall owners. Even if you are not a frequent seller at the markets, many insurance companies offer three-, six- or 12-month policies that you can even pay online. If you only want to attend one market to see how your products sell, you should seek advice from the person overseeing the hiring of the stalls as to your insurance needs.

  You need to think of your stall as your 'place of business'. You wouldn't consider leaving your business premises without insurance, and you should view your market stall in exactly the same way. Your goods are your asset and you need to protect them from theft and damage that may occur in a market setting. With the many hundreds of people that frequent the markets every week, your public liability cover is essential as well.

- **Counterfeiting** Be aware that it's an offence to use a registered trademark without authorisation from the registered owner or authorised user. It's also an offence to breach the copyright of the owners. The penalties imposed under the *Trademarks Act 1995* and the *Copyright Act 1968* allow for fines of up to $55,000 and/ or two years in prison. The Anti-Counterfeiting Action Group, Inc. (ACAG) is an association of trademark and copyright owners/licensees of many brands in Australia and worldwide. You can get further information by emailing acag@tmis.com.au.

- **Pricing your goods** This is where your research of markets and fairs will pay off. Make sure you've carried out comprehensive research into the prices of similar products at other venues. Your products may be amazing and chances are they took many hours to create. You need to factor this in to how you will structure your pricing and whether the eventual price will mirror the cost of the end product and the time it took to make it.

- **Profit margin** In order to be successful and have confidence that your product has a long-term future, you need to add a certain profit margin to it. This is to ensure that even if you sell your products at the wholesale price (what it cost you to manufacture it) to a buyer, you will still cover your costs and make a profit. This profit may only be tiny but at least it will mean that your time and money weren't spent for nothing.

Calculate your price questionnaire

By now, you probably have a clear idea of your ultimate goal with your product. Here's a short questionnaire to get your brain ticking on the subject of pricing:

1. What is the total cost to make your product?

$ _____

2. What is the retail value of this product?

$ _____

3. What percentage mark-up is this? _____

4. Amount of time spent to make the product

_____

5. Price of the market stall and any other fees associated $ _____

Stall design and layout

Market shoppers are usually looking for bargains, but if they can't get them they'll still be happy to pay a good price for quality products. A neat, well-set-out display of your products can only be a positive for your business. Many of your potential customers won't even consider glancing at your stall, let alone purchasing an item, if the stall is chaotic and overcrowded. Your goal is to create a stall that not only enhances what you sell, but also displays the quality of your work. Here are a few simple tips:

- **Consider your stall's signage** Make sure your business logo and signage are visually pleasing, clear and easily recognisable, and that they complement your product. Having eye-catching signage could mean the difference between a buyer stopping for a look or just walking by without a glance.
- **Make adequate space** You might have the best products in the world, but if they're taking over the stall to the point that buyers can't see or touch them, then many won't even bother trying to get a closer look. There's nothing worse for a market-goer than feeling overwhelmed by just looking at the chaos of a stall.
- **Don't give too much space** This can be a big turn-off as well, so make sure you have a good selection of your product to fill the tables and shelves in the allocated space. It's probably a good idea to do a mock stall arrangement before the actual day of the market. This will give you an opportunity to set your products out to see how things will look before the real market day. Make sure you take a quick photo if you really love the display you've mocked up. That way, you can replicate your masterpiece exactly without the stress of relying on your memory.

- **Use a lightweight stall** Unless you have a wonderful friend or relative who is going to be with you at four in the morning for set-up and then again at the conclusion of the market, you're going to want to be as savvy as possible with the materials that you need for your booth display. It needs to be easy to transport and as lightweight as your products can handle.

- **Think about display equipment** You'll need to consider how to feature your product in the best way. If you are selling fashion, you'll need to consider a mirror and changing area. If you are selling bags, you may require some fillers for the insides so buyers can see the volume they will hold. If you are selling jewellery, you may require a locked viewing display case or the appropriate display hangers.

- **Dress for success** If you look like you haven't bathed for days, potential customers may not even bother approaching you or your stall. Dress in a manner that is appealing to buyers without scaring them away. Make sure you look the part of the confident and successful vendor as well as feeling comfortable in your attire. Market days can be long and draining, so it will be important that your clothes and shoes are comfortable.

- **Pack snacks and drinks** I know I sound like a mum, but remember to pack some food and water to see you through the day. You may not have the opportunity to leave your stall for more than a quick toilet break, so make sure you are stocked up with nutritious snacks and plenty of fluids. Being alert is the key to a successful day at the markets. Any sign of fatigue will be written all over your face and it could spell disaster to your success as a marketeer.

Making the sale

Having a stall at a market or fair is very similar to having a traditional store. The customer enters the premises and starts browsing. In some cases they are looking for assistance and in others they may want to be left alone to peruse the shelves and racks without a salesperson bothering them. Whatever the scenario, at some stage you are likely to come into contact with the customer and either offer guidance or opinion, or at the very least have a quick and friendly chat with them. There is nothing more off-putting than a really rude salesperson behind a desk or in a store. I avoid a newsagency that's close to my home because the attitude of the staff is absolutely appalling. Why would I want to purchase my daily newspaper from obnoxious people when I can travel 200 metres further down the road and get a warm smile and a 'have a great day'?

The success of your stall has also got a lot to do with your manner and ability to communicate with market-goers. Like most situations in life, some people are born communicators, while others will avoid any type of contact or conversation with strangers. Chances are the more confident you are with your product and your stall, you'll probably find that talking to customers will come naturally after the first few people show some interest. Just remember, they are stopping at your booth for a reason and it's part of your job to sell your product to the best of your ability without being too pushy or over-the-top. Before the market, prepare some interesting and appealing points about your product in your mind if people ask any questions. Buyers love to know that their purchases have a special meaning, so highlight the key selling points and really impress your customers.

Advertise your brand

A stall at a market or fair is the perfect opportunity to advertise your products and build up brand recognition. Just because you're not a bricks-and-mortar store doesn't mean you can't have brochures, business cards, a website and every other marketing device available to promote yourself. The more your business name is out there for people to see, the better it spells for growth of your business! Don't be afraid to pop a business card in the bag when a purchase is made or to have an old-fashioned brown paper bag stamped with your business name to give that personal touch to your customers. Promoting your product should not be thought of as 'just another thing to do'. It's fundamental to the development of your brand that you endorse how fabulous it is.

Be nice to your neighbours

As a stall trader, remember you have neighbours that have just as much right to be at the market as you do. Treat their space with as much respect as you would hope they'd give to you. Don't encroach on their area or distract them from making sales. It will be worth your while to be friendly because it's nice to know that you have someone to watch your stall when nature calls. A friendly neighbouring stall owner can also let potential customers know that you will be returning promptly to assist with sales.

Testing the waters

There are other ways to sell your products without too much direct contact with your clientele, especially if you don't have the courage or confidence to set yourself up at the markets. Etsy is a social commerce website focused on handmade and vintage items, as well as art and craft supplies. There's a broad range of products, including art, photography, clothing, jewellery, edibles, bath and beauty products, quilts, knick-knacks and toys. Many individuals also sell craft supplies like beads, wire, jewellery-making tools and much more. There is only one rule to follow with the vintage items on the site: they must be 20 years or older. The site follows in the tradition of open craft fairs, giving sellers personal storefronts where they list their goods for a fee of $20. It has been described as 'a crafty cross between Amazon and eBay'.

Etsy has a home-based blog site to help you navigate your way and discuss aspects of the official store. The blog is dedicated to showcasing all of the unique and gorgeous Australian handmade and vintage products, as well as providing resources and support for sellers and buyers. Take a look at australianetsy. blogspot.com.

A crucial factor in the longevity of your business is the length of time it takes to make your product. When I was in my short-lived patchwork pillow phase, it took me about four hours to make each one, which meant selling them at $40 each. This translated into about $10 per hour just in labour. To add insult to reality, I still hadn't factored in the costs involved in producing just one pillow.

Make sure it's worth your valuable time and effort to make your product. Nothing positive will come of spending hours and hours producing your products if you then calculate your earnings as a pittance. This can also be a fast track to giving up on your dream totally. Your product may just require more research and development into how you can manufacture your products more efficiently and with less expense. If you are considering giving up your day job to pursue your dream, make sure you factor in any overheads. Overheads are fixed expenses such as utilities, telephone, insurance and accounting fees. In order to keep your pricing competitive, you'll need to try to keep your overheads as low as possible. Generally, you should calculate your overheads at 20 to 25 per cent of your labour and material costs.

Designing from scratch

At this moment, right across Australia, there are possibly thousands of women trying to break into the market with their ideas or product designs. Many will attempt for years to get that one lucky break, only to have the door closed in their faces more times than they care to count. It's very disheartening for some, whereas others pick themselves up, dust themselves off and start all over again.

Not everyone is going to love your idea as much as you do — unless, of course, it's amazing and revolutionary and it rocks the world. I applaud all those who have gone on to be successful and have had the wonderful opportunity to see their products in stores and on the pages of magazines. I appreciate that behind these products are women of persistence, dedication and patience. For some, it does happen overnight; for the majority there are years of blood, sweat and tears before they hear that magical 'yes'. Like most things in life, hard work, perseverance and commitment eventually pay off. I guess that's why we really need to applaud and support the businesswomen who push through the negativity, hold firm to their beliefs and actually make their dreams come true.

Another embarrassing story

We've all had embarrassing moments in our lives that we wish we could just forget. Some of these situations may be brought upon by ourselves, while others are the unfortunate result of circumstances beyond our control. This is a true story and one that I had completely erased from my memory until recently. During the time of the 'patchwork pillows' fiasco and the 'walkin' the dog' phase was another embarrassing little gem that I'd completely forgotten about, until I unexpectedly bumped into a store owner recently. I was at a trade fair and a man tapped me on the shoulder and introduced himself.

'Hayley, you probably don't remember me, but I work at Peter Baker-Finch Homewares in Brisbane.' As he spoke, a shocking recollection came screaming back into my consciousness.

'I didn't know whether to say hello to you because I always felt bad that I hadn't given your paintings a go in the store,' he said with a hint of sympathy delivered through a down-turned smile.

'Don't be silly,' I said. 'I wouldn't have taken them either — they were hideous. Anyway, great to see you again,' I said, while literally power-walking away from the situation.

I found a quiet area and stood there trying to remember exactly what I had been thinking back in those days. I'd truly forgotten that I had approached a beautiful and renowned store in Brisbane with my crappy paintings. I do remember cramming my car with poorly painted watercolour drawings of butterflies and flowers that looked as if they were done by a six-year-old. I'd purchased the cardstock and paints from a discount store but the paintings were expensively custom-framed. Was I completely bonkers? When I arrived home from the trade show, I ran down to the garage to see if I had kept any of the paintings. Lo and behold, there were my disastrous watercolours in one of those plastic crates. I had to dispose of them immediately, which gave me an immense sense of relief that no longer was there any evidence that they'd ever existed. I was also very angry that I'd wasted so much money on beautiful frames. This is a perfect example of thinking that you have an incredible design idea, only to come crashing back to reality because, basically, the beauty and wonderment only ever existed in your own mind.

Heed my advice and save yourself the time and the possibly immense embarrassment of approaching a store owner by testing out your products and designs on others

first. I've learnt from the watercolour paintings debacle —
and so can you. Remember these four important points:

1. Your products or designs must be of a high standard
and quality

- Get your friends and family members to be brutally
  honest with you. My paintings had no quality and no
  standard. I didn't show anyone my paintings before I
  headed off to see the store owner — a big mistake.

2. Realistically price your product

- I paid about $70 per painting for framing on my
  paintings; the paints and cardstock probably totalled
  $5 (bad quality). Retailers will generally add 100
  per cent to the wholesale price before they put it on
  the shelf. This means that even if I sold my paintings
  to the owner at $100 (I'd make $25 per painting —
  yippee!), he would then have to sell one for $200!
  I can assure you that no one would pay more than
  about $2 for these 'works of art'.

3. The quality of the store you're approaching should
match your design

- Why on earth would I approach one of the most
  gorgeous stores in the city to sell my paintings? The
  'greatness' of my designs was a complete figment
  of my imagination. That was quite obvious when I
  recall the bewildered look on the owner's face when
  I propped up one of my paintings on the counter.

$4.$ Stick to your strengths

- I am definitely no painter or seamstress. In fact, I have no talent in either of these areas whatsoever. Make sure you concentrate your energies on your strengths, not your weaknesses.

Case Study: Sarah Cocker

Sometimes in life, you have the opportunity to meet people that change the way you think. I had the amazing honour to meet Melburnian Sarah Cocker, one of Australia's up-and-coming new designers. Sarah's Ask Alice stationery range has taken the industry by storm and I was fortunate to steal a little bit of her valuable time to delve into her creative young mind. Sarah is the perfect example of a talented young person who had the desire and passion to excel and the business nous to make it work. Here's my interview with her:

SARAH COCKER

ASK ALICE

Have you always been inspired to design and be creative?

Yes, always! Creating things makes me feel complete. When I'm not creating, I feel very flat. I need to be creating things in the same way that I need to eat and sleep, I guess! I try to take a creative approach with everything I do, whether it's baking cakes, designing stationery, writing letters or solving problems. Creative thinking seems to help me achieve my goals. I think the right side of my brain steers the ship.

Has it always been a dream to do what you are doing now? If so, did you need to travel or study to further your creativity and knowledge of the industry?

Yes. I'm so excited to have the opportunity to do something that I absolutely adore. I've always wanted to do something I love for a living and have dreamt of having my own business where I create a product of some kind. I love making all types of craft. I love to knit and draw and make paper collages, so I guess you could say my goal was to incorporate those fun things into my job. I started out with three years of intense study at RMIT (Royal Melbourne Institute of Technology) in fashion design. I then enrolled in the Applied Design course that was offered to me by the fashion department. This meant that I was on top in my fashion degree as well as majoring in business studies. Although I'm not working in fashion now, I don't think there was a more suitable course for me to study. It pushed my work to a whole new level and taught me to put my creativity to work in every area of my life. In my final year, I realised that the fashion industry wasn't a great match for my personality. After graduating, I saved up some money and went travelling for three years — what an incredible, life-changing three years they were! I learnt and experienced more in those years of travel than I did during my three years of study.

My clever mum has a stationery importing and distribution company that she started in the garage of our family home about 15 years ago. Over the years, she has shaped her business into one of Australia's leading stationery distribution companies. During my time overseas I attended lots of trade fairs on her behalf. It turned out that I was good at identifying new products for her to import and I soon found myself being responsible for choosing some of her top-selling ranges. I learnt quite a lot about the stationery industry through Mum and am in awe of her incredible business mind and achievements.

How important is it to have the support of family and friends?

My family and friends are the be-all and end-all of my life. Their encouragement and love for my work is very important to me. My mum is such a role model, and in my eyes she's the businesswoman of the century. Without her guidance and support, my Ask Alice range would probably be a collection of handmade cards that you might find at the local Sunday markets! Mum has educated me about the industry, as well as passing on all the lessons she's learnt. This has been crucial to the growth and success of my business and I can see that she enjoys teaching me as well. The process of getting Ask Alice off the ground was far from easy and there were many times when I started to think it was impossible. At these times it was the help from my family and friends that kept the project on track.

I always test my new designs on friends and family to get their feedback. They always encourage me with stories about where they last saw Ask Alice range or how they were given one of my designs for their birthday. A friend even told me a story about how he was at a dinner party where a girl was talking about this great new sketchbook she had. It turned out that it was one of mine! These stories are my little rewards. They keep me going. It's almost surreal to think that my designs are actually out there in people's homes!

Has it been difficult to create and manufacture your own products?

I knew when I started this business that it wouldn't be easy. You always hear people say 'it's not so easy', so I was expecting quite a bumpy road. I was not prepared for the level of difficulty involved. Turning Ask Alice from a dream into a reality was a lot more difficult than I ever could have anticipated. The reason it was so difficult perhaps comes from the same place that has made my range a success. I've had four golden rules that I set on day one and I've refused to break them. They are:

1. Use environmentally safe materials.
2. Design with intuition and attention to detail.
3. Keep production local and fair trade.
4. Keep costs as low as possible and prices affordable.

These four rules really threw a spanner in the works. The easy option would have been to take production of the whole range to China and print onto non-recycled paper. It would have halved the price of manufacturing. The turnaround time would be much quicker and the whole process would have been a lot easier.

After obtaining a quote from a printer in Melbourne, where I firmly stated that the cost price on my notebooks would be $20 per unit retail, I started to think that China was my only viable option after receiving the printer's feedback. I was heartbroken. I couldn't see any point in continuing with Ask Alice if I couldn't adhere to my four golden rules. I decided at this point that I had two options — give up or keep trying. So, after many visits to many printers, I eventually found one that was willing to work with me and was just as determined as me to make Ask Alice a success. Things appeared to be on track finally.

We launched at a trade fair and had a fantastic response. We took lots of orders and explained to our customers that the range would be ready for delivery in four weeks' time. From that point, it took 12 whole months to get the range finished! I couldn't believe it and I found this period extremely difficult to get through. I was under lots of pressure with all of the outstanding orders and I was worried that people would start cancelling their orders and looking elsewhere for a new product. After lots of problem solving, patience and hard work, Ask Alice eventually came together and the response has been phenomenal.

People really appreciate the fact that the range is locally made, environmentally friendly and reasonably priced. My four rules stemmed from my own ethical beliefs, and as it turns out, I'm glad to share these beliefs with many of my customers.

What inspired the Ask Alice range?

The range was definitely inspired by the time I spent in Japan. When I arrived there, I instantly thought that I would never leave. I was totally inspired by the amazing culture and the incredible aesthetic of Japanese design. The craft stores in Tokyo are out of this world! I collected all kinds of pens and beautiful papers, and I literally felt like I was in a stationery wonderland. My best friend in Japan called me Alice because I would often refer to his country as a 'wonderland', and that I felt like Alice from the story. For the entire two years I lived there, I didn't notice the chaos that consumes Tokyo. In fact, they were two of the most peaceful years of my adult life so far. I had a sketchbook that I took everywhere and filled with scribbles and collages. After filling two thick books with my ideas, I decided that I was ready to turn my collages into something more. I proposed the idea of a stationery range to Mum, as well as the idea of her being the distributor. Her encouragement and confidence in the idea made me very excited and I've been working on Ask Alice ever since.

Do you have any advice for women hoping to break through with their own designs?
I think my advice extends to both men and women. Right from the start, ask yourself about your ethics. Figure out what it is you want your designs to represent. Write down your own golden rules and refer to them every time you start to lose your way.

What's the most important thing you have learnt?
It sounds so clichéd, but never give up, even when things seem impossible.

www.askalicestationery.com; askalicestationery.blogspot.com

What's new?

If you're spending many hours stitching, sewing, drawing or creating and you think that you have what it takes to start a fantastic new career, then some of our wonderful cities have started a great new concept especially made for you and your budding career. With the handmade revolution happening in kitchens and living rooms across the country, it's now become big business and quite a profitable venture for entrepreneurs everywhere. Not only do Melbourne and Brisbane embrace and support the handmade community through a variety of different markets and fairs across the state, but a new concept in retail has been born to assist up-and-coming designers. In 2007, glassblower Isy Galey started a wonderful, new and inexpensive retail option to support designers and artists in her own city of Melbourne called In.cube8r. The In.cube8r concept allows designers to rent glass display cubes and shelves for display of their designs and products. This quirky yet appealing idea has now been franchised to a store in a trendy inner-city suburb of Brisbane, with another about to open its doors in Sydney's Mosman. Most of the artists, ranging in age from 19 to 60, now have the opportunity to showcase and sell their wares without the need to have their own retail outlet. Brisbane's store offers 90 glass cubes for designers to sell their re-vamped, handcrafted and innovative products. Designs and items include everything from T-shirts, jewellery, crocheted and knitted items, remodelled furniture and homewares to gorgeous paintings and sketches. The rental fees on the cubes, shelving and rack systems vary in price depending on the duration of the rental agreement plus size of the space. If you don't have time to devote to markets or fairs, this is an exciting and affordable option to test the viability of your design concept. When I visited the In.cube8r store in Brisbane, I was completely blown away by the products on offer. The items were quirky and often 'one-offs'. Another great benefit is that there's no commission on items sold. The artist receives 100 per cent of the retail price. Check out the fun and interactive gallery at www.incube8r.com.au.

Check out these amazing design websites for more inspiration:

- **www.etsy.com**
- **www.madeit.com.au**
- **www.ethikl.com.au**

My little tips

- Markets and fairs are a great way to test your products before you start mass producing.
- Market-goers are discerning — make sure your products are A-grade and your customer service is the same.
- Do your research in terms of pricing — you want to be competitive.
- Make sure your stall is clean, neat, easily accessible, and that everything is arranged and in order.
- Seek professional help re insurance and public liability.
- Above all, be organised — market day should be taken seriously. And be friendly too — it could mean repeat customers.

Hiring Staff

To employ or not to employ

It goes without saying that by the time you open your doors for trading, you will have made some decisions about the need for employees. It comes down to the nature of your business and whether or not its success depends on the size of your store or your service. Maybe you're a website designer and you'll work alone in a home office for most of your working life. Or maybe when you open your retail outlet you find you're so busy that you can't afford not to hire more staff. You'll be hoping to employ reliable, loyal, trustworthy people, but where are they hiding and how can you find them?

I know from experience that the perfect employee is not always going to walk through the front door, so as far as hiring staff is concerned you have to go with your instincts. You won't always get it right either. I've had some staff members over the years that I thought were great, only to have them let me down in a couple of weeks. I've employed teachers with many years of full-time experience and they would ask for a certain amount of hours per week, which I would duly provide. Some would call in sick on their first day or say that they had a flat tyre. Alarm bells would start ringing loudly in my ears. I gave them the benefit of the doubt, but 99 per cent of the time my initial concerns were justified.

I like to think that I'm a pretty laid-back boss and I do give potential employees every opportunity to consider the role they are taking on before I start shuffling other employees' shifts around to accommodate them. My worst situation came when I had a teacher who was working as a casual and she expressed her need for full-time work. She was a brilliant teacher and I didn't want to lose her, so I did everything in my power to find the hours for her. After the entire reconfiguration of my weekly employee timetable, and a week of organising all my employees to fit within their required hours, she lasted three days and told me she had found work in a legal practice answering phones. Hello? I remember standing there completely dumbfounded for at least a minute — that's quite a long time when someone is standing in front of you waiting for a response.

There were so many things that bothered me about this situation. My main issue was the fact that I had gone out of my way to reorganise my entire teaching structure to accommodate her. I'd annoyed other employees and I'd informed hundreds of parents that she'd be their new teacher and how wonderful she was ... yada, yada, yada. Even writing about it now makes my skin crawl! Of course, there are so many wonderful staff members to help cancel out these bad experiences. They're the ones who walk through the door, day after day, with big smiles on their faces.

With experience, you'll begin to understand what works for your business and what doesn't. Every person applying for a position has an agenda and this will undoubtedly change from month to month. Stay on your toes and don't panic if you get a call 10 minutes before your store is about to open informing you that your employee has unfortunately 'slept in'.

Always keep on the front foot in terms of what's going on in your employees' lives too. It certainly doesn't hurt to keep in touch. For example, if you have university students working for you, find out when their exams and holidays are during the year. That way, you can plan for them to be away at certain times or they may be able to take on extra shifts during uni breaks.

Some employees like to add drama to the workplace, so watch them carefully. Their behaviour can be unsettling for other staff members. Be calm, consistent and firm; you're the boss after all. If some employees get a whiff of a waver, they'll exploit it to the max. Others are unpredictable, so be open and prepared for all eventualities and I'm sure you'll get through. It's tough stuff! It will probably seem overwhelming at the start, but believe me it does get easier. It's truly amazing how fast you become an expert at predicting the behaviour of your employees.

Hiring the right people

I did most of the hiring of staff in the first seven years of the business because I liked to control who was going to be looking after the children in the water. In the past year, with commitments interstate, I've left the hiring and firing to my brilliant and dependable administration manager. Our industry is quite small and it certainly requires a lot of decisions made on an instinctive level above all else. Some people walk through our doors with 20 years' experience in teaching but unfortunately don't have the personality required for the job. A person with only a year's experience might edge in and take the prize because they're bursting with confidence, enthusiasm and a commitment to learn.

Don't settle with just 'anyone' that walks through the door for the interview. You'll have different requirements for different jobs. For example, some employees will deal with customers face to face and others will process orders over the phone. Either way, it's always going to work best if you consider a broad range of candidates rather than being hasty because you're desperate to get someone onboard. I'm, without question, guilty of employing staff because I was desperate to have someone in the pool teaching — sometimes desperate times mean taking desperate measures. Just be mindful that careless staff choices could lead to the untimely downfall of your business.

Above all you want consistency with staff members, not only for the success of your business but also for your own sanity. Customers appreciate happy and familiar faces, as well as staff that know them by name and know how to meet their needs. A constant change of teachers at a swim school is a big no-no. Young swimmers need trust and continuity when they're having lessons. Sometimes the unpredictable happens and employees need time off, so try to have a back-up plan if possible.

All business owners would put the hiring of great staff as one of their top priorities. The ideal situation is to have competent, reliable and cheery staff working for you, rather than being weighed down with the stress and worry that your employees are actually driving your customers away. Customer satisfaction is paramount to the success of a business, but not all business owners are aware that bad staff can sabotage all that hard work in a second.

For instance, my husband and I went out for dinner not long ago. Greg ordered salmon for his main meal and asked the waitress if it could be cooked medium to well done.

'We don't cook the fish a certain way. It's all just served as is,' she replied.

'But you need to cook the fish first, right?' he replied, a little perplexed.

'I know, but it's just cooked all the same. Fish is fish,' she answered with conviction.

'No, it can be cooked a certain way, particularly salmon. Some people like it barely cooked so it's nice and pink inside and others like it done a little more.'

'Whatever ... I'll go and ask.' She turned abruptly on her clunky black Doc Martens, looking very put out that my husband, the physiotherapist, knew more about the food than she did.

It was certainly a bizarre conversation to have with someone that should have known better. The lesson to learn from this experience is to make sure that staff members have a personality that suits the business and ensure you give them adequate training so that they can competently carry out their duties. Outline your expectations for their behaviour while they're at work (for instance, the customer is always right!) and that there are consequences for rude or substandard customer service. Only good things can come from being vigilant with the standard of your staff when you're hiring for your business.

Don't think that the whole recruitment situation is going to be a pushover, either. Sometimes good people are in short supply. Take my industry for instance. The time and season have a lot to do with how many applicants we're going to snag. In the hotter summer months, when children are being placed into swimming lessons right across Australia, you would think that there would be hundreds of eager swimming instructors looking for a job. Wrong! It's the exact opposite, actually. The norm is that instructors have already found firm jobs within the industry and as a result numbers are in short supply. However, by the time winter comes around and there are fewer children attending swimming lessons across the country, instructors tend to lose hours and there's an abundance of instructors floating around (pardon the pun), but no jobs.

Make sure you have a back-up plan if no one applies for an advertised position. If it means you have to quickly train your mum or someone trustworthy for the time being, then do so until you find the right person. Recruiting can be very testing at times and you really need to be on top of things. Stay focused and positive above all.

In my opinion, the best method of interviewing prospective employees is a face-to-face interview. You cannot possibly conduct a job interview over the phone. I made a really big business boo-boo once when I hired a lovely lady over the phone, mainly because I was quite desperate for a teacher and needed one the following day. Her experience as an instructor was very impressive, she sounded well educated and very personable, and lived within walking distance of the school. What a bonus! I thought I'd struck 'employee gold' when I got off the phone. The following morning I received a phone call from one of my staff and the conversation went something like this:

'Um … Hayley, we have a problem with the new swimming teacher,' my receptionist stated timidly.

'What's the matter?' I asked with closed eyes, waiting for the bad news to hit my ears.

'She's a bit ... short — actually "tiny" might be a better word. She can barely get her head above the waterline.'

'Come on, are you guys having a joke with me because you knew how excited I was about her?' I asked.

'Unfortunately, this is not a joke. She's agreed that her height poses quite a risk in the water and she's left after the first lesson block. She said that she hadn't actually worked in anything but a wading pool that was about half a metre in depth and that she hadn't thought that her height would restrict her in the water. The good news is she's lovely and very personable and would be great on reception.'

'But I don't need a receptionist! I need someone in the water teaching and I needed them yesterday,' I frantically replied.

This was, of course, my fault entirely and I take full responsibility for it. I spoke to the lovely lady afterwards and she admitted that she knew her height would be an issue but she hadn't anticipated the depth of the water. Anyway, there were no hard feelings on either side, but I did learn another important business lesson when it comes to hiring: a sit-down, face-to-face meeting is the only way to go.

Starting the hiring process

So where are all those great employees hiding? Think back to your last job interview and where you saw the advertisement. Gone are the days when the only way to find a job was in Saturday's newspaper. Business owners now have many options when it comes to finding potential staff. There are specific places to advertise for staff depending on your industry. For example, I wouldn't advertise for swimming teachers in the *Financial Review*. (I don't think I need to explain further.)

An important part of the swim school is our front-desk position. This is the point of contact for our customers and children and their parents are greeted when they come through our doors. It's especially important that the person at the desk is happy and helpful to our customers, as well as having basic administration experience. I've never in the history of the business advertised for this position. It's not because the same person has worked in that position all the time we've been open either. I've always simply put a little note on our front counter saying we're looking for staff and we've always managed to nab a wonderful mum who attends the swim school. You don't have to spend hundreds of dollars looking for great staff. There are less expensive ways to broadcast a position. Be innovative!

Get it on paper

I still go down the old-fashioned route when advertising for staff — the Careers section in the weekend newspaper. It's always worked for me, so why change something that's still working? If you decide to take up the option for recruitment through a newspaper, take the appropriate amount of time to think about what your particular ad will convey. Here's an example:

SALES REPRESENTATIVE
— Marketing Leaders NSW

A global leader in marketing and business strategies is searching for talented and enthusiastic salespeople to join their team. This is an opportunity to join a creative business brand where you are given support and training to enhance your selling techniques. Previous experience selling marketing is viewed favourably.
Email: adamwalker@marketingleaders.com.au or phone: 0400 000 000.

1. Start with a bold heading stating the job title.

2. Add a subheading to attract attention.

3. A description of the position, the responsibilities and any qualifications, certificates or licences required.

4. Include contact details for your business, including a contact name.

You've placed your ad, so now what? You basically wait for any potential employees to start calling or emailing, but I wouldn't suggest waiting by the phone or staying on the computer, particularly if you have placed an advertisement in the employment section on Saturday. Not all people jump out of bed on a weekend to look for jobs. In fact, most of my job seekers contact me over the next two weeks.

Make sure you have your diary with you during this time so that you can note down names, contact numbers and possible interview times. Mark out clearly the specific times and days you've already set aside for interviews. Nothing spells 'disorganisation' better than when an employer can't tell job applicants their interview time or whether they should bring documents along.

I've prepared a simple form for you to print out so that you'll be ready for applications. Keep the completed forms in a safe place and don't lose them. I have a close friend who performed an entire day of interviews only to lose all the paperwork and have to reschedule the applicants. Be on top of everything and keep all paperwork safe and secure in the one place.

Toni's Cakes and Bakes
INITIAL CONTACT FORM

Date: _____

Applicant's name: _____

Address: _____

_____

Transport: _____ Has own: _____

Hours able to work: _____

Meeting time and day: _____

This is a simple yet effective way to get just enough information before you meet the applicant. It will differ from your actual Interview Form (see p. 228 for a sample form). After you've agreed on a time and date to get together, you should think about the type of person you require for the job. There's no use interviewing someone without really knowing what you are looking for in an employee. This will also help when it comes to preparing interview questions. For example, one of my top priorities is to hire people who live within close proximity of the swim school. We open early and it can pose big problems when six parents and their babies are waiting for a teacher stuck in traffic on the other side of the city. I've stuck with this requirement, even if it's meant rejecting some good people. I've learnt from experience that it's better to have my employees close by. If 'distance from workplace' is a concern, you have to weigh up whether the applicant is worthy of the job.

It's trial and error in some cases and you'll learn through experience the types of people and personalities that work well for your particular business.

Remember, in order to protect yourself from any allegations of bias or misconduct, it can be useful sometimes to have at least two people present when conducting an interview. Some questions are deemed unlawful, so please make sure your interview questions relate closely to the job description. Refrain from asking too many personal questions also. Applicants should bring any references they have from previous employers. If they cannot provide written references, it would be a good idea to ask for a phone number and contact name of their most recent employer or supervisor.

Here are some useful websites for background information and also to answer more specific questions:

- www.wagenet.gov.au
- www.business.gov.au
- www.workplace.gov.au

The interview process

I think a face-to-face, sit-down interview is best for both employer and employee. I think you can judge within minutes whether a person will suit your business and be able to work as part of a team. Keep in mind that the recruiting process is nerve-racking for the applicant. Most will feel a little intimidated or nervous during an interview, so take this into consideration. When I was auditioning for the hosting role for *The Biggest Loser*, I was told after my fourth audition that they knew I was right for job after the first, but they'd been worried about how nervous I appeared in the interviews. I was crazy with nerves and this nearly blew a wonderful chance for me! Fortunately, they did give me the benefit of the doubt by allowing me a few extra chances to calm down.

If you sense some nerves but can see some real potential, then conclude the interview and schedule another one in a few days. Do everything you can to put them at ease during the process — polite chitchat, bad jokes — anything, basically. After you've established some calm, start conducting the interview by going through a full job description with them. Don't sugar-coat anything either.

Go into as much detail as possible about what the job entails and what you expect from them. Give the applicant an opportunity to ask any questions relating to the job and its requirements. Hopefully by this point all cards will be on the table and you'll know whether there's a possibility of a working relationship.

This would be an ideal opportunity to give them potential 'scenarios' that might give you an insight into their personality and their ability to cope in different situations. For example, one question I ask potential swimming instructors is, if a parent started to abuse them for not paying full attention to their child, how would they respond? Think of questions that relate to your particular industry.

Towards the end of the interview, ask the applicant about their goals for the future and where they see themselves in a year or two. If they tell you that they hope to study overseas in the next six months, then you know you may not be on a winner. (I can never quite understand if a comment of this type shows scrupulous honesty or complete stupidity!)

Before they leave the interview, give the applicant a timeframe in which they can expect an answer, regardless of the outcome. This protects you from a phone call every five minutes if they're particularly keen and gives you time to sort through and consider all the applications equally.

After the interview process is over, it shouldn't be too difficult to narrow down the field. Take the time to ring referees and ask them for any useful information about previous experience, work ethic and general ability. When you've made your decision you can call the successful applicant and give them the good news. Remember to send

Toni's Cakes and Bakes
INTERVIEW FORM

Date: _____

Applicant's name: _____

Address: _____

_____

History of employment: _____

Previous employers: _____

_____

Experience in the industry: _____

Certificates/Licences available: _____

Requiring full-time/part-time/casual work: _____

Transport available: _____

Future goals: _____

Hobbies/interests: _____

Other comments: _____

the other applicants a quick email letting them know the outcome. One crucial lesson I've learnt over the years is never to burn your bridges. Always remain courteous to any unsuccessful applicants because you never know when you may require extra or replacement staff. Keep the details of all ex-staff members filed away also, and make them aware they're always welcome back through your doors. I recently had one of my best swimming instructors move back to New Zealand with her family. I told her that she was always welcome to come back and work for me ... and within six months, she did.

Writing a job description

A job description is a formal list of the tasks, functions and responsibilities of an employee. Typically, it outlines to whom the position reports, the qualifications required, a salary range for the position, and so on. A job description is usually developed by conducting a job analysis, which includes examining the tasks necessary to perform the job. The analysis looks at the areas of knowledge and the skill base needed for the job. Job descriptions usually encompass a number of roles within the position.

The purpose of a job description is to have a clear outline of duties and responsibilities to make day-to-day running of the business as well managed and efficient as possible. They usually include the following:

- guidance and improvement in new and existing responsibilities/roles

- assistance in career progress within the business
- determination of amount of pay per role
- expectations within the role.

You simply must have a job description written up for your employees from the day they first start work. This gives a clear summary of expectations and helps stop any confusion that may occur during the term of employment. When I did my first stint on *The Biggest Loser*, I had to create brand-new job descriptions for two of my main managers at the swim school. If I hadn't, I would have been completely disorganised. A job description allows you to manage your staff because it clearly states the duties they are expected to perform. I know my staff prefer to know exactly what their responsibilities are, and what I expect from them in return. All staff, whether you have one or one hundred, should have their duties comprehensively outlined to help avoid conflict and tension. Some employees with similar job descriptions may overlap in responsibilities, especially if they're on the same shift. This sometimes results in a situation where neither employee completes a particular task. Try to head this off at the pass by suggesting staff alternate in taking on the duty, say one week off and one week on. It will make for a calmer and happier workplace if you resolve these issues before they become real problems.

Create your own job description template to suit the particular needs of your workplace (see p. 231 for a simple template to help get you started). Ideally, come up with a document that can be tailored to meet the requirements of each employee (to cut down on your workload). Include all the employee's duties, even if they seem small

Toni's Cakes and Bakes

JOB TITLE: **Store Manager**   DATE: **25/1/2012**

BASED AT: **43 Rose Rd, Roseside NSW 2666**

REPORTS TO: **Joanna Stewart — Store Owner**

JOB PURPOSE SUMMARY: **Outline the general nature and purpose of the job. Offer a brief description of duties and responsibilities. Keep it brief.**

JOB DUTIES: **Outline and break down duties into defined categories. This is can be as comprehensive and as detailed as possible, with daily timelines included if necessary.**

JOB DIMENSIONS: **Outline the scale of responsibilities and the areas to which responsibilities extend — include staff, customers, territory, products, equipment, premises, etc.**

WORKING CONDITIONS: **Outline the terms and conditions of employment, e.g. work from 9 a.m. to 5 p.m. weekdays; One-hour lunchbreak; public holidays granted; may work overtime with paid compensation.**

EMPLOYEE SIGNATURE: DATE:

EMPLOYER SIGNATURE: DATE:

and insignificant. When you've completed each job description, sit down and discuss each section with the staff member. Considering you're probably starting with less than 15 employees, keep your job descriptions simple and easy to follow. You don't want to bombard new staff with a 100-page document or they may just turn and run the other way.

Job descriptions: points to avoid

- Don't put 'targets' into the job description. This is nothing to do with the actual description of the employee's job and responsibilities.
- Don't make it too wordy.
- Remember it's a description of the job, not a workplace agreement.
- Don't spend days working on getting it just right. If you feel you're taking too long, refer to these websites to give you some help:
  — www.bestjobdescriptions.com
  — www.businessballs.com/jobdescription.htm
  — www.ourcommunity.com.au

Testing time

So you've found your employee and it would be a good idea to let them know by phone that they have secured the position. Invite them in for a meeting to discuss the terms of employment and any other questions they may have. Keep in mind that all candidates are going to promote their assets during an interview. It's only when you get some people in a workplace environment that you see their personalities change quite dramatically. I once hired a sweet girl that was so lovely in the interview and then turned out to be quite overbearing and angry when she was put under a little bit of pressure. It's perfectly above board to have a probationary period to see how a new employee performs. The period of time can vary, but at my business we give a minimum of 20 hours' training in the water with one of my current instructors and then they commence on a 'starting wage' for three months. If they show consistency and loyalty to the business, I increase their wage and generally offer them more shifts. Trial or probationary periods may not be right for all businesses, but many find them effective.

My little tips

- Don't expect the perfect employee to walk through the door. Make time for training and motivating your staff — they can't know exactly what you want without your guidance.
- If your initial instincts about a potential employee are not positive — do not proceed.
- All interviews must be face to face. Over the phone or sight unseen interviews can be fraught with disaster.
- Take lots of notes during the interview.

- Have precise job descriptions for all of your staff. This will help avoid any confusion between employers and employees.
- Make certain staff know everything about your service or product. There's nothing more embarrassing than when a staff member can't answer a question about your service or provide assistance with your product.

Managing Your Staff

How to manage staff effectively

Evaluating staff

Training and development

My little tips

How to manage staff effectively

I don't want to start off this section by making excuses for myself, but I think never having had a proper job or full-time employment before I owned the swim school meant I was always playing catch-up with proper staff etiquette. The etiquette of a professional athlete was head down and work your butt off! You don't have much opportunity to slacken off, have a laugh with your fellow team-mates or socialise in general. I probably could have if I'd wanted to, but I can't remember being anything but utterly and completely exhausted and just wanting to spend as much time sleeping and being away from the pool as possible. As a consequence, I'd get to the pool no earlier than I was required to and I would leave as soon as I had finished the swimming session. This, of course, excludes the time when a lovely 15-year-old boy — my future husband, Greg — caught my eye and then I happened to spend extra time loitering. Apart from that diversion, things generally functioned like this — job to do, get it done, on to the next thing.

For as long as I can remember, I always had something I needed to do, or should be doing. I think this is why I don't like to get wrapped up in the entire BS that seems to follow life in general. And let's be honest, the BS is everywhere. Some people seem to create tension and unfortunately most small business owners won't know who these people are until they're well and truly entrenched in the workplace.

I remember when I first opened the swim school I was shocked by the speed at which one negative person could create a toxic environment. I also must admit I had absolutely no idea how to handle the situation. Basically, most of my staff members were 10 to 20 years my senior. Shouldn't they know better? Initially, I found some of the employee relationships hard to handle, but I did understand the principle of 'nipping it in the bud' before things got out of hand. When it comes down to it, it's your business and employees should respect each other and your expectations for their behaviour at work. Not everyone is going to get along famously, but everyone needs to be mature enough to work together.

My advice is to stay on top of everything. You can generally tell if there are issues festering below the surface just by sharing the same space with your employees a couple of times in a day. I think most women know instantly when conflict is close by and we seem to want to resolve it. Some issues can't be fixed easily, but the best way to maintain staff cohesion is to keep your ear to the ground and always listen when the need arises.

I currently have two staff members (they know who they are) that cannot, under any circumstances, get along. They both love their jobs but are not prepared to look for employment elsewhere. They have well-defined job descriptions but because of the nature of the swim school, administration and teaching do somewhat intertwine and therefore staff are expected to work together in certain areas. I don't know if it's their star signs or if it's a gender war, but they just do not gel. I was able to manage the situation before getting the hosting job, but because I had to then relocate on weekdays to another state, the situation between them just went from reasonably manageable to quite stressful. It was an absolutely horrendous position.

I felt like I was losing control over my business because two of my staff members couldn't even acknowledge each another. To add to the calamity, a few of my other staff were emailing me to convey the unpleasantness of the whole work environment. The best I could do was to sit them both down and talk through the situation. Towards the end of *The Biggest Loser* filming, the situation at the swim school had peaked. I remember driving home from a 'challenge' we had just filmed in the western suburbs of Sydney, the migraine from hell pumping through my brain, when the first phone call came through.

'If he doesn't go, I will!' shouted Number One employee. In two minutes the second call came through.

'If she doesn't leave, then I will!' stated Number Two.

I was not in the right frame of mind to deal with either of them, so I told them I'd call them both back in less than 24 hours to discuss the matter. This also gave them time to settle down and think about the ultimatum they had just given me. It was terrible! I had never felt so conflicted in my entire eight years as an employer. I needed them both and they were equally important and essential to my business. I knew deep down the one I'd choose to keep, but as it turned out the decision was made the following day by one of them handing in their resignation.

This is a bad situation for an employer, but hopefully you won't be taking on any reality television hosting roles that require you to be in another state for six months of the year! Generally speaking, things at the swim school travel along quite nicely now. Maybe it's the nature of the learn-to-swim industry, but for the most part I think my staff respect me and know me well enough not to cause tension or too much of a fuss.

I think it's important to lay the ground rules when you start to take on employees. Mutual respect between employees and their employer is the key objective. I always make myself available to my staff no matter the situation, but at the same time I'm no push-over. While you can't play favourites with your staff, you do need to play cereal-box psychologist with some; others will require little or no TLC. Workplace relationships are similar to all other relationships. You need to be flexible in your approach. Different personalities require different management styles. You have to work on getting the best out of your people. Sometimes this requires seemingly endless patience.

Make sure new employees have an unambiguous job description. Even if they're just employed to answer the phone, an exact description of what you require from them is essential. It's also imperative that you take the time to go through it together so there can be no confusion about the tasks further down the track.

Reporting incidents

It's a good idea to make a record of any incidents that may crop up every so often. A written record is desirable because recollections of times, dates and conversations often fade with time. Keep a folder at home or away from the workplace if possible. You never know what might 'go missing' when it's needed for back-up. Here is a simple form you could use should the occasions arise:

Toni's Cakes and Bakes
INCIDENT REPORT

Date: _____ Time: _____

Employee's name: _____

Signature: _____

Others present: _____

Signature: _____

Reason for meeting: _____

_____

Response for employee: _____

_____

Action taken by employer: _____

_____

Date to reassess situation/Improvements: _____

Any comments: _____

_____

_____

_____

Alter this basic template to meet your needs. There are many other things that could be included on the form, but remember it's always best to get down as much detail as possible, with the ultimate goal being resolution. There's nothing worse than trying to conclude a matter with no real feeling of settlement.

Evaluating staff

Developing and motivating your staff is a constant process that shouldn't be left to slide. Whether you are constantly overseeing your business or managing it from afar, the best way to grow and strengthen your business is to provide your staff with opportunities to improve. Evaluation of your staff and the feedback you get from them give you greater insight into what may or may not be working within your business.

As an employer, you are also responsible for rewarding your staff. It doesn't always have to be a pay increase (although 99 per cent of employees probably prefer this over anything else), but as any business owner will tell you, you can't increase an employee's pay every time they do something fabulous. Any recognition and encouragement can make someone feel great. This could be as simple as some praise or positive message on the bottom of a pay slip. I've realised that one of the worst transgressions we commit as employers is to never praise staff when they perform above and beyond demands or requirements. I've seen the positive power of letting my staff know how valuable they are. I see the happiness written all over their faces when they know that their hard work has not gone unnoticed. It always makes me feel good about myself too.

Evaluation at work

Evaluating staff doesn't need to be a laborious task. It's entirely up to you how often your evaluations take place, but do make sure you don't leave it too long; this leads to disgruntled and bitter employees. Here is a sample evaluation form you can establish in your own workplace.

Toni's Cakes and Bakes
EVALUATION FORM

Employee's name	Task / Field	Needs attention	Good	Excellent
Michelle Paige	Morning set-up	•		
	Feedback to parents		•	
	Attitude			•
	Attendance		•	
	Efficiency			•
	Knowledge of levels	•		
	Team work			•
	Organisation			•
	Filling in for staff	•		
	Training	•		
	Total	4	2	4

General comments:

Date of meeting with employee:

Training and development

It probably goes without saying, but no matter what business you're managing or operating, you must keep up to date in your specific field. Industries and disciplines are constantly changing, so you will need to ensure that your staff has the knowledge and skills to remain at the top of the field. Your business may rely on employees regularly updating their qualifications and attending seminars. If so, this is a great opportunity for staff to keep learning and acquiring new skills and techniques. Not only will it improve their own skills, but it will broaden their knowledge base as well. For an employer, this is a positive outcome.

Appointing a specific staff member to take charge of training new staff may be useful. This not only takes the pressure off you if your business is starting to expand, but it also gives the appointed trainer an extra level of responsibility. With any business, you can't spread yourself too thinly either. At some stage you may want to have a holiday or you may simply need to spend time away from the business, so it's comforting to know that someone else has the knowledge to train any incoming staff.

Try these techniques for establishing a good rapport in the initial training stages.

- Try putting the new employee at ease on their first day. Smile, chat and relax.
- Introduce them to any other staff that they will be working alongside.
- Familiarise them with their workplace surroundings, including the tea- and coffee-making facilities, toilets, rest areas, etc.

- Give them instructions on how to conduct their specific roles. Make sure you are thorough and precise.
- Don't assume they will know what you expect them to do. For example, if you require staff to fill out their own time sheets, keep their workstations tidy, empty the bins when they leave, then make sure you tell them. It's all part of the training process.
- Give them the opportunity to ask questions.
- If possible, give them an opportunity to practise the task with you present so they feel comfortable.
- Make sure they have an alternative contact point if they have further questions.

My little tips

- Make sure you have regular meetings with your staff to ensure that things are running smoothly and to pick up on any problems early.
- Don't play favourites — this is a fast track to an unpleasant work environment.
- Keep a record of all incidents no matter how trivial.
- Encourage and recognise great efforts by staff members.
- Evaluate staff — this keeps you on your toes as an employer and them on their toes as employees.
- Train your staff on any product changes or developments — the more knowledge they possess the better.

Legal Obligations

Employer obligations

Workers' compensation and OHS

Anti-discrimination: your role

Pay as you go

Superannuation Guarantee Scheme

Awards

Structure of employment

Annual leave

Terminations and resignations

My little tips

Employer obligations

I won't lie by pretending that I love being responsible for every little detail of my business. Don't get me wrong — I'm all for 'doing the right thing' and 'being there' for my staff, but occasionally it can be extremely draining. Some days it's hard enough being responsible for my family and making sure that their needs are met, let alone having the added responsibility of my swim school.

I'll let you in on a little secret that you may not know if you're new to the game of business. Not only are you responsible for the running, management and success of the business, you are also very responsible for many issues that affect your employees. There ... I've done it! And we're not just talking about the normal legal things that we need to adhere to — I'm referring to EVERYTHING! I realise this may seem a bit dramatic, but I'm quite serious. I learnt this gem after only one day of trading and it took me quite a long time to get my head around it. Nowadays, most employees know their rights at work. You have to be able to pre-empt any nasty issues before they turn into major problems. Make sure that you remain up to date with current obligations and responsibilities in the workplace so they don't come back to haunt you.

The trick to staying on top of things comes down to being aware of situations within your business. Get to know your staff well. It's your responsibility to keep your ear to the ground. In my business, I usually find things out by default. The employer is often the last person to be clued in on current events within the workplace, even though you seem to be there 24/7. Stay vigilant with every aspect of the business, whether it's workplace safety, disgruntled staff or customer issues. Prepare yourself to have loads of patience and allow time to solve any employee-related issues sooner rather than later. If you're new to business, you should ask yourself whether you could cope with a range of issues *before* you start trading. If not, then maybe becoming a small business owner is not for you. Even though I have a manager at the swim school, I still have to contend with issues that are specific to the owner — that's me!

Workers' compensation and OHS

If you have employees, then legally you must have workers' compensation cover (WorkCover in most states). Although it's an added expense to your operating cost, it does buy you peace of mind. Don't presume that staff will never seek workers' compensation or that your workplace is a safe and accident-free zone. Anything can happen at any time to anyone. I've been very fortunate over the past eight years (touch wood) that only one of my staff members has required workers' compensation and that was for slipping on the pool deck. Obviously, I then installed extremely expensive non-slip flooring over the entire swim school area, but it was money well spent for my customers' and employees' safety. Anything you can do to allay safety concerns in your workplace is worthwhile, because it lessens the worry for you. When I was hosting *The Biggest Loser* I had to be away from the swim school for about five months. I almost made myself sick with worry that safety measures wouldn't be maintained. It should become second nature to check everything within your workplace to ensure the highest safety standards. You can't be at work all the time, so you need to be diligent about occupational health and safety (OHS).

Here are good reasons to maintain the correct health and safety policies in your workplace:

- a policy will ensure that the appropriate safety procedures are in place;
- it will ensure that your employees are guided towards taking the necessary actions in relation to safety;
- it will define safe and unsafe behaviour in the workplace;
- a policy should outline exactly how Occupational Health and Safety (OHS) issues should be dealt with;
- a policy should define who is responsible for safety matters within the workplace.

You need to keep in mind that employees may also seek compensation for issues that aren't so easy to categorise. An injury resulting from a fall at work is easy for the employer to see and a doctor's report can be issued. However, other situations are harder to define. Two important examples are stress-associated illnesses and workplace bullying.

Did you know that more Australian workers are making psychological stress-related compensation claims than ever before? It's estimated that the national cost of such claims is around $105.5 million per year.

Stress

Stress-related illnesses can come about by:

- work overload, sudden increase in the workload or working long hours;
- poor management practices and procedures;
- organisational change;
- workplace conflict or breakdown in communication, bullying or gossip;
- job insecurity;
- internal competitiveness between employees;
- pressures from outside the workplace.

Bullying

Workplace bullying is when you are verbally, physically, socially or psychologically harmed by your employer or another person or group of people at work. It can happen in any type of workplace and is often similar to that found in a school playground. Psychological and social bullying can include:

- verbal abuse or making fun of your work or you (including your family, sex, sexuality, race or culture, education or economic background);
- excluding or isolating you from people or situations;
- psychological harassment (playing mind games, ganging up on you);
- intimidation (making you feel less important or threatening you);
- giving you pointless jobs that are unrelated to your job;
- giving you impossible tasks that can't be achieved in the given time or with the resources provided;

- deliberately changing your work roster to make it difficult for you;
- deliberately holding back information you need to get your work done properly.

Physical bullying or violence is when you are physically attacked or threatened. It can include:

- pushing, shoving, tripping or grabbing;
- punching, kicking, scratching, biting, spitting or any other type of direct physical contact;
- attacking or threatening with equipment;
- any form of sexual harassment;
- physical symptoms of stress such as headaches, backaches or sleep problems.

It's also worth keeping in mind that bullying and conflict are not the same thing. Disagreement and conflict happen in most workplaces. They should never be allowed to turn into bullying or harassment.

Stress-related issues and bullying should never be swept under the carpet in the vain hope that they will right themselves. It could easily cost your business a great deal of money if a successful lawsuit is launched against you. Damage to the reputation of your business and the overall morale among existing staff could be irreparable, not to mention the fact that your reputation in the community could take a battering also.

Problems may still arise, even if you are the most diligent of employers. Take comfort from the fact that OHS legislation throughout Australia deals with workplace bullying and stress-related issues, and will guide you through issues as an employer. To find out more, simply go to the following websites:

- www.ohshandbook.net.au
- www.careerone.com.au

To ensure you have the appropriate and necessary cover for your business contact the following state- and territory-based authority:

- Australian Capital Territory: www.ors.act.gov.au/workcover
- New South Wales: www.workcover.nsw.gov.au
- Queensland: www.workcoverqld.com.au
- South Australia: www.workcoversa.com.au
- Western Australia: www.workcover.wa.gov.au
- Victoria: www.worksafe.vic.gov.au
- Northern Territory: www.worksafe.nt.gov.au
- Tasmania: www.workcover.tas.gov.au

Workplace safety tips

1. Have an emergency evacuation plan. Make sure your employees are made aware of it and that they've signed the appropriate documentation to say they have been shown.

2. Comply with any permits or storage requirements for any chemicals or liquids.

3. Have a safety file on the premises for all relevant documentation (for example, incident reports).

4. Conduct your own safety inspection once a week and keep on file any issues that need to be addressed before they becomes hazards.

5. Have the necessary insurance cover in place.

Anti-discrimination: your role

Your first foray into small business could be cut dramatically short without the appropriate procedures and policies in place. This includes your responsibility for prioritising a written policy on discrimination and harassment in the workplace. Don't become complacent or adopt the attitude that it won't happen in your workplace. There is an increased potential in small businesses for issues of discrimination and harassment to occur if there's no policy in place. The first step is to have the necessary policy and procedure organised from the start of trading. You should then appoint yourself or another senior person of authority to look after any discrimination and complaints. Contact employer organisations, small business associations or industry associations for assistance in relation to anti-discrimination laws.

Pay as you go

Pay as you go (PAYG) is a system that allows businesses and individuals to pay instalments of their expected tax liability from employment, business or investment for the current income year. The system calculates an annual income on the basis of a weekly or fortnightly payment. The appropriate level of taxes and payments are then withheld and passed on to the Australian Taxation Office (ATO). For employees with only a single job, the level of taxation at the end of the year is close to the amount due before deductions are applied. Discrepancies and deduction amounts are declared in the annual income tax return. Refunds are made after the annual assessment. A refund may also go towards reducing any taxation debt that may be owing. The withholding tax rate for an employee's primary job is lower because a tax-free threshold applies. Secondary employment will be taxed at a higher rate because the tax-free threshold has already been applied to the primary job.

PAYG Withholding Tax is:

- made to employees for salary and wages;
- made under a voluntary agreement where a business and a worker (a contractor or subcontractor) enter into an agreement to withhold amounts from payments made to the worker. The worker is not an employee and they must have an Australian Business Number (ABN);
- made under a labour hire arrangement where a labour hire firm engages a worker to provide labour to another business. The worker is not an employee of the business or the labour hire firm;

- made to a supplier who has not quoted their ABN;
- made to an investor in receipt of investment income where neither an ABN nor a tax file number (TFN) has been quoted;
- made to a non-resident investor in receipt of investment distributions, such as dividends, interest, fund payments or royalties.

Don't confuse PAYG Withholding Tax with PAYG Instalments Tax. After your business lodges your tax return for your first year of trading, the ATO will calculate an estimate of next year's tax bill. You'll then be asked to pay tax instalments either monthly, quarterly or annually depending on the estimate. This is PAYG Instalments Tax. I know there's so much to remember and only a few billion brain cells to compute and store it. As a new business you will need to register for GST and PAYG and this can be done quite simply with the help of your registered agent (tax agent or BAS agent). They need to ensure their registered agent number is recorded against your record before they can add a new business account.

Group certificates

A Group Certificate or Payment Summary shows the total payments your business made to the employee and the total PAYG Withholding Tax that was taken out during that financial year. It is a legal requirement that you provide your employees with their Payment Summaries at the end of each financial year.

The PAYG Payment Summary for each employee will include:

- gross income from your business;
- total tax withheld;
- Australian Business Number (ABN) or Withholder Payer Number (WPN).

The information on an employee's PAYG Payment Summary is required when completing their tax return and it is your responsibility to get it to them no later than 31 July.

What are employers' requirements?

- All electronic Payment Summaries provided must be non-editable.
- Payment Summaries must use letter-quality print for legibility.
- Where you are intending to provide Payment Summaries electronically, you need to contact your employees and advise them that they can receive their Payment Summaries electronically or by paper. (You can assume that an employee has agreed to receive their Payment Summary electronically if they do not respond to you by the due date provided.)
- Tell your employees when the payment summaries are available and ensure they know how to access and print them.
- Ensure the method you choose to distribute electronic payment summaries to your employees is secure enough to protect the tax file numbers and other personal

information, and to meet your obligations under privacy and taxation law.

Superannuation Guarantee Scheme

All business owners must adhere to the guidelines of the Commonwealth Superannuation Guarantee Scheme. The premise of the scheme is to create better conditions for all Australians in their retirement. As an employer you have an obligation to pay super contributions on behalf of all your eligible employees. These contributions are in addition to your employees' salaries and wages.

The minimum superannuation amount is 9 per cent of each eligible employee's earnings base. Some employees do not have 'ordinary time earnings'; rather, the basis of their super is another earnings base. This may have been contained in:

- an industrial award;
- an existing agreement they have with their employer;
- a fund's trust deed, or legislation.

If an employee's earnings base changes from quarter to quarter, remember to work out the amount of super you pay in line with the earnings base changes. Once again, your accountant should be able to advise you.

Who is eligible for super contributions?
- Employees aged between 18 and 70.

- Employees paid $450 (before tax) or more in a calendar month.
- Employees who work full-time, part-time or on a casual basis for more than 30 hours per week.

Who is not eligible for super contributions?

- Employees who are paid less than $450 (before tax) in a calendar month.
- Employees who are under 18 years of age and working 30 hours or less per week.
- Employees who are foreign executives holding certain visas or entry permits under the migration regulations.
- Employees who are paid to do work of a domestic or private nature for not more than 30 hours a week (for example, a part-time nanny or housekeeper).
- Employees who are members of the army, navy and air force reserve.
- Employees temporarily working in Australia for an overseas employer and who are covered by a 'bilateral social security agreement'. A Certificate of Coverage must be presented to receive the exemption.

To work out if someone is eligible for super contributions use the Super Guarantee eligibility decision tool found at the ATO's website: www.ato.gov.au.

How is super calculated?

Joanna is an administration officer and is paid $700 per week before tax.

Joanna's earnings base for
   the quarter (13 weeks) $700 x 13 = $9,100
Her employer's super contribution
   for the quarter   9% x $9,100 = $819

When is superannuation payable?

It's important to pay the correct amount of super by the cut-off date each quarter to avoid paying the superannuation guarantee charge to the tax office. This is a fee charged to any employer who does not meet the minimum superannuation payment requirements by the due date on behalf of the employees.

Dates for cut-off

Quarterly payment cut-off date

Quarter 1
   1 July–30 September   **28 October**
Quarter 2
   1 October–31 December   **28 January**
Quarter 3
   1 January–31 March   **28 April**
Quarter 4
   1 April–30 June   **28 July**

If the quarterly cut-off date falls on a weekend or public holiday, you should make the payment by the next working day. You can choose to make super payments more regularly than quarterly. They can be made fortnightly or monthly, so long as the total amount you owe each quarter is paid by the quarterly cut-off dates.

Which superannuation fund?

One of the essential requirements of an employer is to get the superannuation fund details of a new employee. If they have an existing fund, look up the fund's website for information on how and when to pay their contributions. If your new employee doesn't have a superannuation fund, they will need to decide on one and make sure they inform you. Penalties are applied if an employer doesn't make superannuation payments by the required due date.

Awards

An award wage is arrived at through arbitration and is legally fixed by an industrial commission. It is payable to all employees in that particular occupation by law and contains the minimum terms and conditions of employment in addition to any legislated minimum terms. Fair Work Australia (FWA) has responsibility for making and varying awards in the national Workplace Relations System.

Types of awards

Awards in the national Workplace Relations System include two main types:

Modern awards These awards replaced many existing awards and came into effect from 1 January 2010, and have been created under the new national Workplace Relations System. The commencement of modern awards means that there have been changes to minimum terms and conditions for many employees. The changes vary by state, industry and employer.

Modern awards contain terms and conditions about:

- base rates of pay
- overtime and penalty rates
- types of employment
- enabling the employer and employee to agree on an individual flexibility arrangement
- work arrangements (e.g. rosters, variation to working hours)
- hours of work
- rest breaks
- classifications
- allowances
- leave and leave loadings
- superannuation
- procedures for consultation, representation and dispute settlement.

Federal awards These awards (created before 27 March 2006) have either been reviewed or are in the process of being reviewed to see if they should be replaced by a relevant modern award.

In 2010, a third category of awards became part of the national Workplace Relations System. This is a state award covering the employees of non-constitutional corporations (generally sole traders and partnerships).

Contact the Fair Work Infoline on 13 13 94 to find out more about awards. Some employees are covered by an agreement, not an award.

What is an agreement?

An agreement is a legally enforceable document between an employer and employees which contains employment conditions that are often more generous than conditions in awards.

Workplace agreements regarding wages and conditions can be either:

- collective agreements; or
- individual Australian Workplace Agreements (AWAs).

Australian workplace agreements (AWAs) are formalised individual agreements negotiated by the employer and employee. Employers can offer 'take it or leave it' AWAs as a condition of employment. They are registered by the employment advocate and do not require a dispute resolution procedure. These agreements operate only at the federal level. An AWA can override employment conditions in state or territory laws except for occupational health and safety, workers' compensation or training arrangements. The agreement is required to meet only the minimal Australian Fair Pay and Conditions Standard. Agreements are:

- for a maximum of five years;
- approved, promoted and registered by the Workplace Authority;
- operate to the exclusion of any award;

- prohibit industrial action regarding details in the agreement for the life of the agreement.

Structure of employment

As part of the hiring process, you will need to consider the roles your new staff will play in your business. You may be a sole proprietor with no employees, but this may change if your business becomes instantaneously successful. Think about the roles employees will take on in the business. I knew it wasn't a one-woman show when I first started the swim school, so it was imperative that I hire some casual staff at the very least. A few things that I had to consider before employing staff were:

1. How many teachers could fit in the pool without crowding?
2. Could I give new employees enough hours initially?
3. Could my business actually afford it?
4. Could I afford another full-time staff member?

I started my very first week with two full-time staff (myself and the other partner) and four casuals. One month on, we had acquired a part-time employee and another three casuals. Of course, this was based on the fact that we had more families enrol and we also started to trade seven days per week instead of six. Back in those days, the learn-to-swim industry wasn't governed by an award wage, so we had to do a bit of research into what swimming instructors were being paid at other swim schools in the area.

Before hiring staff, look at the Fair Work Australia website (www.fwa.gov.au) to make sure you check any award wages that may be associated with your industry. After that, you will need to consider your requirements. Are you able to do things yourself? Will you be stretching yourself to manage the business by yourself? Can you afford to have another employee? If the answer to the last question is yes, then you will have to consider the following employee structures.

Casual

Casual employees are usually employed on an hourly or daily basis and don't usually get paid sick leave or annual leave. They are paid superannuation based on the amount of hours worked. Casuals generally get additional pay, called a casual loading, to compensate for not receiving sick or annual leave benefits. Casual staff are also less likely to have regular or guaranteed hours of work. Notice periods (the formal notification of time given before termination of employment) do not apply to casuals.

Over the past nine years that I've owned a small business, the majority of my staff has been casual employees. It really comes down to what employee structure is most suited to your business type and what your budget allows. There are certainly pros and cons associated with having casual staff, but the same can be said for part-time and full-time staff. Your aim should be to hire staff based on your current business circumstances. Try not to get yourself into a situation whereby you jeopardise your own wage just so you can support a staff member.

Part-time employees

Part-time employees work regular hours each week, but generally their hours are fewer than full-time employees. They usually receive the same basic entitlements as full-timers, based on the hours worked (this is called pro rata). Any accrued entitlements such as annual leave should be paid when the employee leaves. If they're dismissed or made redundant, they may be entitled to notice of termination or payment in lieu of notice (except in cases of serious misconduct) and redundancy pay.

Full-time employees

Full-time employees generally work 38 hours per week and have a continuing contract of employment. Benefits such as paid sick, annual and long-service leave usually apply.

Annual leave

Employers must generally give all permanent full-time employees at least:

- Four weeks of paid annual leave (five for shift workers)
- Ten days of paid personal/carer's leave per year
- Two days of unpaid carer's leave (when needed)
- Two days of paid compassionate leave (when needed)
- Twelve months of unpaid parental leave

The new Federal Government Paid Parental Leave (PPL) scheme started on 1 January 2011 and replaces the current

**Baby Bonus for eligible parents. The PPL scheme provides
18 weeks' payment at the current federal minimum
wage ($543.78 per week or $9,792 in total). This amount
is a available to all eligible parents — including part-time or
casual employees — who earn less than $150,000 per year.**

**To be eligible for the PPL Scheme, you must have worked
at least 330 hours (the equivalent of 1 day per week) for
10 months in the 13 months before birth. You can find more
information at www.familyassist.gov.au.**

How much is the employee paid? The employer must
pay annual leave at the employee's base rate of pay for their
ordinary hours during the period of leave. This doesn't
include separate entitlements such as incentive-based
payments and bonuses, loadings, monetary allowances,
overtime or penalty rates. On termination of employment,
an employer must pay an employee for any accrued untaken
paid annual leave.

- **Calculating annual leave** Under the National
  Employment Standards (NES), an employee's entitlement
  to annual leave accrues progressively during a year of
  service according to their ordinary hours of work and
  accumulates year to year.
- **Taking annual leave** An employee can take paid annual
  leave when their employer has agreed to their request.
  The employer must not unreasonably refuse to agree
  to a request. There's no minimum or maximum
  amount of accrued annual leave that must be taken at
  a time.

- **Public holidays** Employees who normally work on public holidays are entitled to a day off with pay (subject to reasonable requests to work).

Terminations and resignations

Notice period

A notice period is the amount of notice an employer must give an employee if they plan to terminate the employee's employment. Under the National Employment Standards (NES), an employer must provide a set notice period if they terminate the employment of a permanent employee.

Period of continuous service	Notice period
Not more than 1 year	1 week
More than 1 year, but not more than 3 years	2 weeks
More than 3 years, but not more than 5 years	3 weeks
More than 5 years	4 weeks

The relevant notice period increases by one week if the employee is over 45 years of age and has completed at least two years' continuous service with the employer.

Who doesn't get notice of termination?

- A casual employee.
- An employee engaged for a specific period or task.
- A seasonal employee engaged for a specific season.

- An employee whose employment is terminated because of serious misconduct (for example, an employee that engages in theft, fraud or assault).
- An employee (other than an apprentice) to whom a training arrangement applies and whose employment is for a specific period or limited to the duration of the training agreement.
- A daily-hire employee working in the building and construction industry (including working in connection with the erection, repair, renovation, maintenance, ornamentation or demolition of buildings or structures).

Unfair dismissals

An employee has been unfairly dismissed if Fair Work Australia (FWA) finds that the dismissal was harsh, unjust or unreasonable. They must also find that the dismissal was not a case of genuine redundancy.

It's not an unfair dismissal if the employer is a small business employer, i.e. they employ fewer than 15 employees (up to 1 January 2011 this means 15 full-time equivalent employees) and they follow the Small Business Fair Dismissal Code when dismissing an employee.

What's harsh, unjust or unreasonable?

When FWA considers whether a dismissal is harsh, unjust or unreasonable, they take into account a range of factors including:

- if there's a valid reason for the dismissal relating to the employee's conduct or capacity;

- if the employee is notified of the reason and given an opportunity to respond;
- if the dismissal relates to unsatisfactory performance and whether the employee is warned about it before the dismissal.

An employer has the right to summarily dismiss an employee for serious misconduct. If you need more information, you can call FWA on 1300 799 675 or visit www.fwa.gov.au.

Small business fair dismissal code

There are new unfair dismissal laws for small businesses and their employees under the new national Workplace Relations System.

Special arrangements There are special unfair dismissal arrangements that apply to small businesses. These arrangements simplify the dismissal process. They recognise that small businesses usually don't have big human resource departments to help them, that they can't afford lost time and that it's difficult to find other positions for employees.

Small business employers will benefit from:

- a minimum employment period of 12 months instead of six months (i.e. an employee can't make an unfair dismissal claim in this 12-month period);
- a simple Fair Dismissal Code to help employers ensure dismissals are not unfair;
- a specialist service for small and medium-sized businesses from the Fair Work Ombudsman.

Give a little

You can have the best product or service on the market, but if you don't have the right people working for you then quality doesn't mean a thing. If the members of your staff have high standards and they show respect for you and your business, chances are you'll be a success. It does go both ways though. In order for your staff to work at a high level, they too must be respected and looked after. I have bent over backwards to accommodate some employees, only to be let down. Unfortunately, this may also happen to you at some stage, but through experience you get better at predicting the outcome of certain situations. Here are a few things that I've learnt along the way that my staff appreciated:

- **Remember birthdays**
- **Give constant feedback, both good and bad** Offer solutions and training if the feedback is negative.
- **Always return phone calls, emails or texts from staff members within 12 hours** I don't think I have ever not returned a message within hours of receiving one. This shows that you care about their issues or queries.
- **Listen when you can't listen anymore** You may find that you have some staff that just love to talk to you for the sake of talking. Choose your moments with these people and avoid making them feel 'dodged'.
- **Be a shoulder to cry on** Since becoming a business owner I've realised that although it's a stressful and 24/7 responsibility, there are always people out

there (staff members) that are possibly doing it a lot tougher than you. Be mindful that you could be a tower of strength in their life and someone they rely on not only for job security, but also for support and understanding. If this isn't in your make-up, then try to be open to the concept of developing a softer side. Staff will appreciate it!

Lend me your ears

The Listener: it's by far the most important role I now have in my small business. Because of the nature of my current life — half the year hosting *The Biggest Loser* in another state and half the year as owner of a swim school — my role in the business has definitely changed. I have two managers (teaching and administration) and hardly a day would pass when I don't speak to them both. I very quickly realised in my first season of *TBL* that the only way I could solve issues at the swim school was to listen on the phone and direct from a thousand kilometres away. You may find yourself in a similar situation one day, especially if you have a baby, go on holidays, or simply decide to take time off. You'll have to hand over the reins to someone else while you're away and you have to feel comfortable doing it. You also need an incredible amount of trust in the custodian(s). It's almost impossible to let go completely but the key is to always keep in close contact 'on your terms'. You know the personality of your staff and when it's OK to 'check in'. In the first four weeks of my six-month stint away, the calls were constant. I often wondered how I was going to juggle both roles. The key is to listen, instruct and play 'make-do psychologist' to your staff. I have wonderful staff, but as in most work places they have their tiffs and struggles.

I have absolutely no ability to judge personalities when I'm hiring. I think everyone is lovely and happy and cheery, but when they mix with another staff member, sparks fly. I'm always baffled by sparring and posturing at work. My opinion is that you come to work, you do your job and you do so happily in the knowledge that you're passing on a skill for life. Simple, isn't it? Why waste time on the trivial things? I know there can be tensions between staff members but nine times out of 10, most volatile situations can be averted.

My little tips

- If in doubt, always seek professional advice. A solicitor is your best bet.
- Your business can only be successful if you have complied with all of your legal obligations.
- Don't think stress or bullying can't or won't happen in your workplace — seek advice if you need to.
- Conduct your own safety inspection of your premises once a week. Attend to any issues straightaway.
- An accountant can provide you with comprehensive information and let you know what your requirements are re PAYG tax, super, awards, leave, and general employer/employee requirements.

Mixing Business with Family and Friends

Disaster or success?

Unless you have a bottomless money pit, endless amounts of energy, the best experience in your field and a love of going it solo, chances are high that you'll want a business partner. This partner might just turn out to be a friend or family member. You probably have a close and wonderful relationship with your soon-to-be business partner and it seems impossible that everything won't work out perfectly. Chances are it will be a triumph. But I also want to open your eyes a wee bit to the possibility that it may not turn out so rosy. Without doubt, a working partnership gone bad can destroy a friendship. Either way, decisions still need to be made when you work in a business partnership, even if relations are strained.

When friendships work

Fortunately, I've had both positive and negative 'family and friends' working relationships. I had the amazing opportunity to work with my best friend and we didn't fight or even have a disagreement in the four years she worked at the swim school. I was devastated when she finally left, her love of horticulture too strong to keep her focused at the pool, but I had seen it coming for months. Now when we see each other we talk about everything but business, which suits us just fine. I think we worked so well together because of our mutual respect, coupled with the fact that we weren't business partners having to make difficult decisions together. Trying not to show her any favouritism was difficult at times, but I believe that our personal relationship was never an issue when it came to the daily running of the business.

When friendships don't work

Back in 2002 when I started the swim school, I went into partnership with one of my husband's groomsmen. He was an amazing swimming teacher and he would always talk about his ambitions of owning his own business. He's still a good friend despite the fact that we ended our working partnership about three years into the business. In hindsight, we were both very similar. The swim school was an opportunity for us both to use our years of experience, but in some ways it was just a stepping-stone to our ultimate dreams. Fortunately, my love of swimming and the gorgeous little children (not to mention my binding lease) kept us motivated to continue with the business. When he did eventually make his final decision to start afresh with his own business, the timing was right for both of us.

We certainly had a mix of good times and stressful times. Looking back, we didn't really speak about our goals for the business or its future. I think we were both so excited about starting that we didn't bother to look past the first week, let alone the first year. In retrospect, I can see why he needed to spread his wings and discover other passions and interests in his life. He had been sketching and creating his fashion designs for as long as I'd known him and he'd always had the travel bug. The fact he was an amazing swimming teacher and such a hit with both the parents and the children was a bonus for the business, but without the drive he eventually had to move on. I think it was definitely the best decision we made for the business and the friendship.

I remember quite clearly the day that the 'transfer of ownership' papers were signed and the swim school was finally owned by me alone. I realised how wonderfully freeing it felt to be able to make business choices without having to consult with another person.

Going into a business relationship with someone (especially a friend) is something that you shouldn't consider lightly. You need to evaluate many things before taking the 'partnership plunge'. Do you think you'll be able to handle conflict with your friend if your opinions differ?

Friendship partnership questionnaire

Here are few important questions to discuss before embarking on a partnership with a friend or family member:

1. What are your goals for the business? If they differ, it's probably time to talk things through until you both reach an honest place.

2. How will the day-to-day roster run?

3. How will the business operate if one of you falls ill or needs extended time off?

4. How will you arrange pay?

5. How will profit within the business be divided?

6. Are you both happy with your financial, legal and accounting set-up?

7. What will happen if one of you wants to leave? Have you thought about an exit strategy?

8. What is your current family or personal situation? Are there any plans to start a family? If so, how will this work?

9. Do you both have definite job descriptions? If so, these need to be finalised and written up before the business starts trading.

10. Have you completed a mission statement? If not, why not?

Put all your cards on the table before the business starts. Even the best of friends have their differences. When those differences start to impinge on the business, the problems may be magnified. Don't be naïve about how well you know a friend. Personalities can change quite quickly when the pressure is on, so don't presume that problems can always be avoided easily.

Be honest with one another from the start and make sure that you have back-up plans or strategies to face certain situations. It's crucial that you both have similar goals and

targets for the business. If you differ wildly about these goals then you'll both find yourselves in a dismal working situation. Organise a meeting to go through all the things that may be concerning you. Don't feel that you can't be completely honest about your concerns. You may find the meeting tense and uncomfortable, but it simply must be done. It's better for your relationship and for the business to talk things through in a calm and structured way.

Case study: Larraine Bilbie & Sarah Bowe

I can't begin to explain how completely magical it felt when I visited this gorgeous little gift shop, located in one of Brisbane's prettiest areas, to interview Larraine and Sarah. I've travelled extensively and this store still proves to be one of my favourites. Nestled in a popular shopping precinct since 1992, this quaint store has become one of *the* stores to visit. The soft lighting and floral scents create an intoxicating ambience, even in the unbearable heat of a Brisbane summer. Coming Up Roses creates an exquisitely peaceful haven for those who appreciate whimsy. I've been shopping here since the store first opened and I've always enjoyed my little chats with this dynamic mother-and-daughter team. I've often wondered how they managed to have such a successful personal and working relationship. I was on a mission to find the secret to their success.

My first impression of this duo was their love and passion for the business and the amazing respect they have for each another. Coming Up Roses started as a furniture business for Larraine and husband, Roy, back in 1992.

Over the years, more gifts and homewares were added. These days, the furniture has disappeared and mother and daughter keep the store looking gorgeous with all the latest retail trends.

Sarah lovingly and meticulously maintains the buying side of the business, attending trade fairs in various states a few times a year. She's quick to point out the importance of remaining 'on the ball' with trends and changes within the retail industry. The internet has made it significantly easier to track the latest fads and styles. Her keen eye for the 'new and fabulous' is without doubt the driving force behind their store's success.

Both Larraine and Sarah pride themselves on maintaining a high level of customer service and the product range entices clientele from far and wide. Both admit that they share a quirky sense of style, which makes it incredibly easy to agree on product ranges. They've also been able to maintain a working relationship that's quite separate from their mother–daughter ties. There's not a lot of shoptalk outside of the business and both have realistic and comparable goals for the future. The shop is very important, but family and life balance seem to override the business.

Coming Up Roses certainly has a positive vibe. Larraine admits that you need to be on your game constantly in small business because you can't afford to have a bad day when you've got customers to look after. They've built up a strong customer base over the years and I get a sense that they pride themselves on a store that markets a personalised product. They don't bother with traditional advertising but instead offer free gift-wrapping and postage, which has encouraged loyal patronage and a large dose of goodwill. Word of mouth is also a positive force. These strategies have been so successful that they've been able to spend their advertising and marketing budget in other areas. As an example of the power of the personal touch, my husband is a repeat visitor to the shop and admits that the free wrapping is definitely a drawcard for him.

Both Larraine and Sarah agree that their employment and management program could have been better established and developed over the years. Their decision to operate with a small team of staff served them well in the early years. However, as the business continued to grow this approach has meant that they've both had to spend long hours at the store during the frantic months.

They've had their share of life-changing events too. Both Larraine and Sarah have suffered life-threatening illnesses, but they had to carry on with the business although at times it was stressful and tiring. Both agreed that owning a store is not as glamorous as it may appear. Larraine admits that a lot of work goes into making the shop look effortlessly stylish.

Owning a well-established business in difficult economic times can be challenging for even the most savvy of business owners, but Larraine and Sarah have advice for all the budding female entrepreneurs out there. Here's what they say:

- Love what you do. This is without doubt *the* most important aspect when going into business. You need to be able to imagine surrounding yourself with your product for years and years to come.

- If it's a partnership, have respect for one another and have similar goals for the business.
- Keep work separate from any relationship outside of the business. Have a healthy work–life balance.
- Have set tasks within the daily running of the business.
- Be prepared for the busy times if you're starting a seasonal business.
- A great location is a must.
- If the budget permits, invest in a cleaner and an ironing service. This small weekly or fortnightly investment could mean a few extra hours spent with family and friends.
- Above all, stay ahead of the pack.

Larraine and Sarah's scorecard

Top Marks for ...

- Innovative and 'current' products
- Merchandising in store is alluring for customers
- Personalising their product (free gift-wrapping and postage)
- Superb customer attention
- Fantastic location
- Lovely owners
- Great store layout
- Support for local fetes and charities

Areas for improvement

- Staff training
- More time for themselves

When it doesn't work with family

I don't want you to get the wrong idea about me. I can work with friends, as I've demonstrated with my all-time BFF. Our personal friendship was never compromised by our working relationship. I realise the same can't be said about my husband's groomsman, but this wasn't a bad falling-out, more a case of a 'different directions'.

I've worked through quite an interesting six months with my sister Joanna, however. I love her to pieces but we are polar opposites when it comes to business and managing people. I should have known it was going to be like riding a roller coaster, but I lined up for the thrill anyway. Was I totally insane? Looking back, the whole situation came about because my sister had decided she was quitting her high-flying corporate job to focus on being a mother. For as long as I could remember, Jo always loved to be in control and she was very good at it. She was completely focused on climbing the corporate ladder and she did very well in the male-dominated industry she was in. Everyone in a our family was a little shocked when she made the decision to quit, but following the death of our older sister we'd all decided to become more family-oriented and our goals had shifted.

Needless to say, after a few months Jo was getting itchy feet. Both her children were at school but she was quite adamant she wouldn't put them in after-school care. Unfortunately, there aren't a lot of jobs that start at 9.30 a.m. and finish at 2.30 p.m. — how wonderful would that be? Around about the same time, an administration position came up at the swim school for a Sunday morning shift. It was only four hours in length but Jo was excited to start, even though she was way too qualified for the job and it had absolutely no managerial requirements. It was basically a front-desk job — answering the phone and marking off children's names as they came in for their lessons — and could not have been further from her corporate job if she had searched for it. This was a long step down compared with what she was used to doing in her previous, high-pressure job. She promised me that she wouldn't be bored and happily accepted the lack of responsibility and management demands with open arms.

I was thrilled. Not only had I helped my sister out, but I knew she was more than qualified, extremely personable, and above all I didn't have the stress of trying to fill the difficult Sunday shift. Win, win and win! Life was working in a mysteriously convenient way for once — and I relished it.

Not too long after she started, cracks began to surface. Jo thrives on being in charge and making all the decisions, but unfortunately I was the one in charge at the school. I think some of my staff were so used to my laid-back approach that they were completely thrown off-guard by Jo's more corporate approach.

In hindsight, Jo has amazing instincts when it comes to efficiency, getting the job done and maintaining high standards in a workplace. Coming from the stressful work environment that she was used to didn't quite translate to the laid-back, easy breezy workplace that I maintained.

I should have known it wasn't going to go 'swimmingly'! Jo is very protective of me and takes her role as big sister very seriously, so having the roles reversed was a little awkward. Fortunately, there were no major incidents, but we both agreed that we'd rather be sisters than co-workers. Not too soon after, Jo became pregnant with her third child and gave notice to finish up. Phew! Catastrophe diverted!

There were no hard feelings between my sister and me, but it did teach me a very valuable lesson: don't mix business with family members. This is my personal point of view formed from my experience, and it really does depend on your situation. I really should have gone with my gut instinct, but I think deep down I was really *hoping* it would work.

If you are thinking about going into business with one of your family members, consider your current relationship and concentrate on the problem areas (if there are any) or simply think back to the times when you've had disagreements. How have these situations been resolved? Who attempts to resolve the matter? If the answer is you, how will you feel when a situation arises and you're the one that's trying to smooth things over? Believe me, when business is involved, the gravity of certain situations is magnified. Problems need to be sorted out then and there, especially if there are other employees at the workplace. You don't want your staff knowing that the bosses are at odds.

Take some time to decide whether going into business with a family member is really worth it. If it's purely financial (a 50 per cent split means 50 per cent less capital that you need to put in), will it really be worth the headaches that may come?

My little tips

- Being best friends outside of the workplace doesn't always carry over into a work environment.
- Honesty is the best policy. Always nip things in the bud before they get out of control.
- Before you go into business with a friend or family member, have a discussion and plan how to solve any issues that may pop up.
- Keep work separate from personal relationships.

Structuring Your Business

Different legal structures

What is an ABN?

Four business structures

My little tips

Different legal structures

When you start your own business, things are not always going to be straightforward and simple to understand. I have a financially savvy husband, but he suggested I sit down with an accountant, a bookkeeper and a solicitor to go through the best structure for my business. I advise you to do the same. You need to get your head around the legalities of owning your own business and many budding entrepreneurs come unstuck at this stage of the process.

Unless you are a small business guru or already have a trusted financial advisor, it will pay to get professional advice to set you on the right path. Maybe you'll simply go over the accounting, tax and legal options associated with your business. Don't be discouraged if it all seems too hard to follow. My poor brain was on information overload trying to process the difference between a company and a family trust. After a short time, however, things begin to fall into place. There will be more involved if you're entering the business with a partner, and that's why it's imperative to get the help of a professional. While all this may seem unnecessary and mind-numbingly dull, there are legalities to be met also. Believe me, you'll be thankful that you had the right structure in place if you're entering a partnership.

There are obviously advantages and disadvantages within all business structures. There are fewer headaches for sole traders, however, which is great news for some.

The structure you eventually choose will depend on the size and type of your business, along with your personal circumstances and how much you want to grow within the business. You should also consider a certain amount of flexibility too, as you may want to change the structure to suit your needs further down the track.

The key is to ensure that the structure you decide on is well and truly in place *before* you start the business and that you're able to comply with various legal requirements. This is where your bookkeeper or accountant comes in. Laws change from time to time and it will be a load off your mind knowing someone will educate you about any changes. It may be wise in some cases to connect with a taxation consultant who specialises in your particular industry. It's essential that you understand the responsibilities of being a small business owner.

The way you set up your business may affect the following:

- the way tax applies to your business
- the protection of your assets
- your business operating costs
- how other businesses deal with you
- what you feel comfortable with and gives you peace of mind.

Please keep in mind that I'm not a qualified accountant, solicitor or legal advisor, so the information provided should be used as a guide only. I highly recommend that you meet with a professional before you proceed further.

What is an ABN?

The Australian Business Number (ABN) is a unique 11-digit identifier for all business dealings with the Australian

Taxation Office (ATO). It identifies you with the ATO and other government departments and agencies.

When will you use your ABN?

- Dealing with the Tax Office (the ABN is quoted as a reference).
- Dealing with other government agencies.
- To make sure that other businesses don't withhold tax at the top marginal rate from payments they make to you.
- When supplying goods and services to other businesses (and other entities carrying on enterprises).
- To register for the Goods and Services Tax (GST) and to claim input tax credits and Fuel Tax Credit (FTC).
- If you want to be endorsed as a deductible gift recipient and/or you want to be endorsed as a tax concession charity or income tax exempt fund.
- To account for or offset your taxation obligations on an activity statement.

For further information and to register for an ABN, you should visit the Australian Taxation Office at www.ato.gov.au.

Four business structures

There are different ways that you can structure your business. However, these four are the most widely used in Australia.

Sole trader

If you can structure your business as a sole trader, then by all means do it! Many small businesses start out with a sole-trader structure but change as the business expands or they may require financial assistance whereby a 'partnership' agreement is the answer. 'Sole trader' doesn't necessarily mean that the business has only one worker. The sole proprietor can employ others to do any or all of the work in the business. In comparison with corporations and other organisations, the amount of paperwork you need to submit is negligible, but you should still seek professional advice when setting up your business structure.

What is a sole trader?

A sole trader (also known as a sole proprietor) is a type of business entity that is owned and run by one individual and where there is no legal distinction between the owner and the business. All profits and all losses accrue to the owner (subject to taxation). The proprietor owns all assets of the business and all debts of the business are their debts and they must pay them from their personal resources. This means that the owner has unlimited liability. It is a 'sole' proprietorship in the sense that the owner has no partners (partnership).

A sole proprietor may do business with a trade name other than his or her legal name. This also allows the proprietor to open a business account with a banking institution. For example, I could open a business called Toni's Cakes and Bakes. This doesn't necessarily mean that Toni has anything to do with it. I don't have to use Hayley's Cakes and Bakes.

Advantages

- It's simple to set up and there's minimal paperwork.
- All of the rights, obligations and property of the business are in one name, so there are no additional legal requirements to fulfil.
- You retain complete control over the business and all decisions are yours.
- There are no establishment costs.
- There are minimal reporting requirements — no annual meetings, lodgement of returns (except your personal tax return) or passing of any resolutions.
- The income tax rate for the business is the same as your personal tax rate, which means that any business losses you incur can be offset against any other income you might have, such as a rental property.
- You are not considered an employee of your own business and are free of any obligation to pay payroll tax, superannuation contributions or workers' compensation.
- It's relatively easy to change your legal structure if the business grows, or if you wish to cease trading.
- There's no division between business assets or personal assets, which includes your share of any assets jointly owned with another person (such as your house or car). Your liability is unlimited which means that personal assets can be used to pay business debts.

Disadvantages

- Unlimited liability, which means all your personal assets are at risk if things go wrong.

- There's little opportunity for tax planning or income-splitting arrangements.

Legal requirements for sole traders

GST: Sole traders may apply for GST registration, which can be done on the ABN application form. You are required to register for GST if your annual turnover is $75,000 or more.

Drawings: You cannot claim a deduction for money drawn from your business. Amounts taken from a sole trader business are not wages for tax purposes and are not tax deductible.

PAYG: Sole traders generally pay PAYG instalments (Pay as you go) towards their expected end-of-year tax liability. This should be lodged before your income tax return is lodged.

How much tax do sole traders pay? It depends on marginal tax rates. Being a sole trader means you pay the same tax as individual taxpayers, but if your business hasn't had a particularly successful year — or you never planned to earn that much anyway — you may well avoid tax altogether if you earn less than the tax-free threshold — currently the first $6,000 earned. For current tax rates, please refer to the ATO website.

Partnerships

Becoming a business owner comes with a certain amount of risk. Going into the business in a partnership arrangement is, without doubt, another form of risk. Any agreement should not be entered into lightly. Even though it may seem like a great idea at the time to go into business with your best friend, I strongly recommend that you think it over carefully, have serious discussions and put everything in writing before you make any major decisions. It hadn't even occurred to me when I went into business with a friend, that things might get tricky or a little rocky along the way. I hadn't considered that my partner might lose interest and want to move on to something else entirely. While your bank balance or current financial situation might be the overriding factor in your decision to go into partnership, what do your instincts tell you? If your intended business partner has goals for the business that don't align with yours, then you may want to reconsider. It's a lot more difficult to abolish a partnership than a sole-trader structure.

How is a partnership defined?

If you operate your business as a partnership, you're conducting your business with one or more people as partners receiving a joint income (but not as a company). The partnership is a legal structure and all rights, liabilities and property are jointly owned or owed by the partners involved.

Advantages

- Set-up costs are generally low.
- There is privacy of affair. As a partnership, it is illegal for either of you to divulge your partner's business standings at any stage of the business relationship.
- Someone else (or others) can share the workload and the legal responsibilities.

- Someone else (or others) can share losses and legal responsibilities.
- There's a greater management base — two (or more) heads are better than one. A diversity of training, skills, experience, personalities and talent brings strength and flexibility. Many (talented) hands make light work.
- There's more capital to start up the business, which invariably means that there's a lot less stress on your financial situation. More capital may also mean you can buy more stock, advertise more widely, hire an employee or get a better location.
- The income can be evenly divided if the partners are members of the same family. This means a lower tax threshold will apply to each family member's income, reducing the total tax payable.
- The income that the business generates is shared between the partners and therefore any losses that the business incurs can be offset against the income of the partners.
- Joint liability means that creditors will have stronger security for any business loans that may be advanced to the partnership.

Disadvantages
- Conflict can arise between partners. This can destroy a relationship that you may have thought was unbreakable.
- If one of the partners decides to leave the business but the other party wants to remain, a 'buy out' figure should be reached, because the partner that remains may have to find some quick finance to settle the deal. This is not a desirable position for the 'stayer'. If you

don't have any equity, then your only decision is to find a
line of credit or you may have to sell the business if you
can't afford to keep it.

- If you are able to buy out your partner's share, consider
how many hours they devoted to the business and the
types of duties they performed. You may have to find a
replacement for them. If they were the powerhouse of
the operation and had become intrinsic to the smooth
running of the business, then this may be more difficult
than you think. If they were a dud, you might be able to
take on their duties or employ someone to take on their
role. Think about this before you start trading. You can
possibly draw up an agreement to reflect the roles each
partner performs and the time and effort they invest.

- Divided authority is another big downer. Partners can
have differing views about the direction of the business
and where it should head in the future. Lack of shared
purpose may pose a problem if agreement can't be met.

- There are costs associated with concluding a
partnership agreement.

- Making the transition from 'partnership' to 'sole trader'
can be a little daunting, for example, all decisions rest
with you, there may be less capital if your partner had
been contributing, and there is no one to share the costs.

- You can lose private assets such as your home, contents
and vehicles to settle debts of the partnership.

Partnership variations

You should also keep in mind that that there are three
variations within the 'partnership' structure to consider.
These are general, limited and joint venture.

General Partnership Partners divide responsibility for management and liability, as well as the shares of profit or loss according to their internal agreement. Equal shares are assumed unless there is a written agreement that states otherwise.

Limited Partnership and **Partnership with limited liability** 'Limited' means that most of the partners have limited liability as well as limited input regarding management decisions. This generally encourages investors for short-term projects, or for investing in capital assets. This form of ownership is not often used for operating retail or service businesses.

Joint Venture Acts like a general partnership, but is clearly for a limited period of time. If the partners in a joint venture keep repeating the same project or start a different project, they will be recognised as an ongoing partnership and will have to file as such and distribute accumulated partnership assets upon closure of the joint entity.

The partnership agreement

You should not and cannot get away from drawing up a partnership agreement. The agreement should state exactly what each partner's responsibilities are, how the responsibilities are reassigned if a partner should cease to be a part of the business agreement and anything else that you have discussed. A qualified legal advisor can write an agreement for you or you can see an example of one at www.smallbusinessnotes.com.

Legal requirements of partnerships

GST: As a member of a partnership, you can apply for GST registration. You can apply for this on the ABN application form. A partnership must be registered for GST if its annual turnover is $75,000 or more.

Drawings: As a member of a partnership, you cannot claim a deduction for money you draw from the business. Amounts you take from a partnership business are not wages for tax purposes, even if you think of them as wages.

PAYG: Partnerships are not liable to pay PAYG instalments. Instead, you and the other partners may be liable to pay PAYG instalments on the share of income you each receive from each partnership.

Who pays income tax? A partnership is not a separate legal entity and doesn't pay income tax on the income it earns. Instead, you and each of your partners pay tax on the share of net partnership income that you each receive.

While the partnership doesn't pay tax, it does have to lodge an annual partnership income tax return to show all income earned by the partnership and deductions claimed for expenses incurred in carrying on the partnership business. The tax return also shows each partner's share of net partnership income.

Super payments: As a member of a partnership, you are responsible for your own super arrangements as you are not employees of the partnership. You may also be able to separately claim a deduction for personal

super contributions you make. If you have any eligible
workers, you must pay a minimum of 9 per cent of
their ordinary time earnings as Super Guarantee
contributions on their behalf.

Trusts

I had absolutely no idea about trusts many years ago, nor did
I want to know about them. When I was doing research on
trusts for this book, I actually realised how interesting the
structure is from a logical perspective. I strongly advise you
to seek professional advice about trusts and ensure that you
understand it thoroughly. Here's my advice: make sure you
have had a nice big cup of coffee and have had a good night's
sleep before you attend the meeting! I don't have any learning
difficulties that I'm aware of, but I have been known to
switch off if I can't follow things. If you're of a similar ilk, ask
for the simplest possible explanation from the professional
and don't be shy about asking questions. Here are the basics:

What is a trust?

A trust is a relationship where a business is transferred to
a third party who has legal control and has a duty to run
that business to benefit someone else. A trust structure
can be implemented in a business or for trading purposes.
It involves the trustee (usually an individual or corporate
entity) holding certain assets in his or her own name, but for
the benefit of a group of people. This group is referred to as
'beneficiaries'. The trustee is required to use any property
belonging to the trust for the good of the beneficiaries and
not for his or her own purposes. The trustee is entitled to

be reimbursed for expenses, but not entitled to be paid any fees unless the trust deed provides for this and it is agreed upon by all of the beneficiaries.

Trusts are generally created because they allow flexibility and tax minimisation. They can also be a popular way to structure your business because they allow an accommodating means of distributing income and assets. They are considered quite handy as they can provide certain income tax savings by distributing income among tax-advantaged beneficiaries. A trust itself doesn't pay income tax on profits providing that the profits of the trust have been fully allocated to the beneficiaries in the relevant financial year.

There are two main types of trusts — unit and discretionary:

Unit trusts A unit trust is similar to a family trust but it is used for businesses rather than for a trust associated with a family. In a unit trust, the beneficiaries hold 'units' in the trust. At the end of each financial year, income is distributed to the unit holders in proportion to the units that the beneficiary holds. The trustee has no discretion. A unit trust has the ability to be negotiable, which means that you can buy and sell units and it has fixed annual entitlements to income and capital, therefore the trustee cannot reduce these entitlements. Owning units in a unit trust is similar to owning shares in a company, although a unit trust is fundamentally different to a share in a company. A shareholder has no interest in the assets of the company whereas the unit holder has a proprietary interest in all of the trust property. The defining elements of a unit trust are the trustee, trust fund and the unit holders.

Advantages

- The units can be easily transferred and be taken back by the trustee.
- Less regulation than a company.
- In some cases, you gain taxation advantages over a company.
- The unit trust deed can be designed for the needs of the principals and beneficiaries.
- There are no legal issues with redeeming units from the unit holder.
- It's far less complicated to dismantle when compared with a company structure.

Disadvantages

- The units are an asset themselves and therefore a unit trust does not offer the same asset protection as a discretionary trust. If a person is made bankrupt, then the person's units will be treated like any other asset and sold off to acquire the necessary capital to pay creditors.
- Tax-free distributions cannot be made as easily from a unit trust as from a discretionary trust.

Discretionary trusts The most common variety of trust is the discretionary trust. The trustee of a discretionary trust has the power to decide how the profits will be distributed among the beneficiaries. With a discretionary trust, the beneficiaries are identified in a category of individuals none of which has a claim or right on a fixed proportion of the trust's property. Only the trustee has the ability to distribute the income of the trust among the beneficiaries in any way. For example, you can allocate income between members of the family to minimise the amount of tax you have to pay. Be very wary though, as under the Tax Acts, trusts cannot be established for the purpose of avoiding having to pay tax.

Advantages
- The trustee has the power to distribute the profits.
- The trustee has the ability to distribute income.

Disadvantages
- There are costs associated with setting up the trust.
- It may have ongoing costs.
- Additional Management demands. Having assets in a family trust means that you have another entity to manage. It may mean more tax returns to do, and it will certainly require good record keeping and business management.

Legal requirements of trusts

Reporting and paying income tax: Your discretionary trust does not have to pay tax. Instead, the trust beneficiaries pay tax on their share of the trust's net income. As a trustee, you can use your discretion each year to decide which beneficiaries will receive income. Trusts can pay very high rates of tax on any profits that are not distributed.

Super payments: Your trust must make super contributions for any eligible employees. This includes you if you are employed by the trust.

Companies

A private company is a complex structure formed by one or more people who wish to conduct business that is a separate legal entity to themselves. When you form a company, you could become an employee, director and/or shareholder of the company.

Private companies are regulated under the Corporations Law, which sets out substantial obligations for company directors. Establishment and ongoing administrative costs associated with Corporations Law compliance can be high. This is why the structure is generally considered to be better suited to medium to large businesses.

If you operate your business as an incorporated company, the business is a distinct legal entity that is regulated by the Australian Securities and Investment Commission (ASIC).

Advantages

- A company has far greater access to capital for the running of the business.
- A company pays tax on its own profits.
- Shareholders are not liable for the debts of the business.
- There is increased asset protection.

Disadvantages

- A company is more expensive to establish.
- The tax-reporting requirements for companies are far greater than for sole traders and partnerships.
- Shareholders have little say in the running of the business.

Legal requirements of companies

Annual company tax return: Your company must lodge an annual company tax return to report its income and deductions, and the income tax it is liable to pay. All companies must pay their own income tax. A company pays tax on its net profit at a flat rate of 30 per cent, which may be an advantage for businesses with high profit levels.

Wages: If you receive wages or director's fees from your company, you need to include them in your individual tax return and pay tax on them at the individual's tax rates.

Super payments: Your company must make super contributions for any eligible workers it employs, including you as a company director.

Legal status: A company name must indicate the company's legal status. A proprietary company must include the word Proprietary or the abbreviation Pty in its name. A company must also indicate the liability of its members in its name. If the liability is limited, the company name must end with the word Limited or the abbreviation Ltd. You can only choose a company name that is not already registered to a company or business. There's also a list of words that you cannot use without special approval.

Before you lodge an application to register a company, you must decide how the company will be internally managed. For more information about business structures and responsibilities, you should contact the Office of Fair Trading in your state or territory.

My little tips

- Seek advice from people in the know if you are not sure about what business structure is best for you.
- Create the structure before you start trading.
- Although business structures and legal responsibilities may seem tedious and boring, your responsibilities should not be shirked or put to the side.

How Much Money Will You Need?

Show me the money

Unless you have a crystal ball lying around the house, it's virtually impossible to predict exactly how much money you'll need to start your business and how much it'll take to keep it going. Over the years, I've known many women who have dreamt of starting their own businesses, and even went as far as researching and writing their business plans, only to arrive at the dreaded 'finance' section and call it quits. It really is a massive reality check when you realise how much start-up capital you require, plus the added cash flow just to keep the business alive.

Certainly, having prepared a business plan will put you in a better position to understand the amount of money required. Keep in mind that your predicted operating budget may just be that — a prediction. Some elements within your start-up budget may be fixed amounts — things such as rent of premises, hire and lease of equipment, loan repayments, insurance, etc. Others can vary dramatically from month to month depending on growth or reduction in your turnover — wages and superannuation, electricity, merchant fees and the cost of stock.

Bear in mind that the first 12 months are a teething stage in terms of how much money you will turn over and spend. During this time, hopefully you'll be see the peaks and troughs of your business, which will then allow you to organise your budget with more confidence.

After my first year of owning the swim school, I realised (obviously) that the winter months (June, July and August) were quite significantly slower than the summer months. This allowed me to budget more efficiently by putting more classes on during the warmer months and fewer classes on during winter (read: less wages to pay out). Your business may not be quite as seasonal, but your potential customers may be buying up big in November and December, but not so much in January and February. This is a situation where only time and on-the-job experience will tell. You'll quickly realise that the busier and more fruitful months have to hold up the leaner months.

If starting a small business has been a lifelong dream, then you don't want to find yourself waking up in a cold sweat because you're worried about raising enough finance. Take it from me — I've started a business from scratch and also bought an existing business, and in both cases I needed to be financially sound. The last thing you need is to make yourself financially vulnerable before your doors even open. If there was ever a time to take a reality check, it's right now! Be really honest and think about how a new business venture may impact on your current financial situation. If you are up to your eyeballs in debt, then possibly waiting a few months (or years, depending on your state of affairs) may be the only sensible decision you can make. Don't get me wrong. I'm all about taking risks, but only up to a point! Try to remember the reason you're starting the business in the first place. I'm quite certain it's to fulfil a dream and hopefully continue on through life feeling happy and satisfied. I'm sure it isn't to feel stressed out and worried every day because of the financial stranglehold the business has put on you.

Having the appropriate financial support is without question the key to longevity and strength in any small business. Just as important, if not more so, is getting the right financial advice. Obviously, I have no financial background or expertise, but I can steer you in the right direction. Thoroughly researching your options will be time well spent. There are many issues to consider before you start sourcing finance options. Here are some of the important ones:

Can you provide any security?

The bank will want to know what assets you can sell in the event you default on your loan. They generally assess your current position on the four C's of lending:

1. **Character** Applying for a loan with a bank manager or loans officer is similar to a job interview. They will be assessing your personality and character to ascertain whether you are confident and self-assured and that you have a positive and definitive goal for the future and longevity of your business.
2. **Cash flow capacity** Are you going to be able to repay the debt confidently? Do you currently have the cash flow to support the repayments?
3. **Condition** What are the current economic conditions in your area of business?
4. **Collateral** What security can the bank use as a warranty to safeguard themselves if you're unable to make your loan repayments?

How much money does the business need to start up?

Presumably, you have a good idea about how much finance is required to fund your dream before you go to a financier. In some cases, this may be particularly difficult to determine, so a bit of guesswork may be required. Either way, there are two elements to consider when doing your sums:

1. **Fixed capital** refers to the items needed to run your business on a daily basis, for example, the premises, plant and equipment, any machinery, etc. Other fixed items may be cash registers, merchant facilities, office equipment or shop fit-out.
2. **Working capital** refers to the money required to fund your business on a daily basis, for example, wages, superannuation and stock.

Sample monthly operating budget

Expenses	Projected monthly expenses
Advertising	$500
Office supplies	$75
Wages	$3,990
Superannuation	$298
Payroll taxes	$394
Rent	$3,500
Loan repayments	$600
Utilities	$700
Insurance	$550
Bank fees/merchant fees	$330
Telephone/fax	$300
Leased equipment	$250
Accounting fees	$100
Stock	$880
Depreciation	$100
TOTAL	$12,567

What will the borrowed money be required for?

First you need to thoroughly categorise what you need financially and how you'll spend it. Prepare an operating budget and this should help you establish how much money you are going to need to support the business. You need to determine whether it should be short-term or long-term finance.

Short-term finance This encompasses the money required to buy stock for the business, any raw materials and basically any other working capital needs. In this case, your method of financial support may be via an overdraft facility or a creditor. Here are some things to remember:

1. It generally needs to be repaid within 12 months.
2. It's self-funding, meaning it is usually used to purchase assets that will generate the funds to pay back the loan when they are sold.
3. It can be used to purchase items that will be quickly turned over in the business.

Long-term funding This encompasses the money required to fund any fixed assets, property, vehicles or other business assets. In this case, your method of financial support may be via a bank loan, hire purchasing, leases or mortgages. Here's what is required:

1. Applications for loans may require a comprehensive business plan or mission statement, at least three years of financial statements and predicted business forecasts. Expect to get a drilling! Remember: banks aren't

handing out money like they were pre-GFC (Global Financial Crisis), so expect to be assessed down to your last cent. If you are buying into an existing business, the bank may also require the profit and loss statements and financial statements to assess their viability and worth.

2. A business owner's assets that are purchased using long-term funding need to create an amount of money that should sufficiently cover the principal and interest repayments and hopefully also make a profit above this.

3. Hire/lease — this may require you to provide proof to the company that you are not a credit risk. You may also be required to put down an initial deposit for the equipment, and repayments are regular instalments of principal and interest.

4. The terms of either personal loans and term loans should be understood before you proceed. Personal loans are generally three to five years and can be used for the purchase of stock (depending on the amount), shop fixtures and fittings or business vehicles. Term loans are repaid by regular monthly instalments of principal and interest. These loans are typically used for purchasing the premises or land, buildings and large equipment. Unlike personal loans, term loans can generally operate on a cycle of one to 10 years.

Business angels

An angel investor or angel (also known as a business angel or informal investor) is an individual or organisation

that provides capital for starting up a business, usually in exchange for convertible debt or ownership equity. A small but increasing number of angel investors organise themselves into angel groups or angel networks to share research and pool their investment capital.

Thousands (maybe more) of women across Australia would love to start their own brilliant and innovative business, but simply have no capital behind them to get things off the ground. You may be in a similar position, thanks to the GFC. This is where Angel Investors can come in very handy. According to the Australian Association of Angel Investors (AAAI), almost $2 billion have been invested by over 15,000 Angels over the past few decades. You simply have to find the organisation or individual that can see future potential in your idea.

If you are seeking an investor, AAAI will ask four basic questions:

1. What is the business or employment background of the key players in the business? This gives the investor confidence in your ability to run your business. This information will also assist them to see how their skills, experience and contacts will complement yours.

2. What is your business? Describe what you have been doing up till now.

3. What are your short- and medium-term plans and opportunities?

> $4.$ How can an investor help? Many investors want to assist in more ways than cash investment. They have skills and contacts that can assist you to reach your goals quicker than you could on your own.

For a more comprehensive overview of angel investing, visit the AAAI's website at www.aaai.net.au.

Here are some other great organisations that can give advice about start-up capital:

- www.australianinvestmentnetwork.com.au
- www.yourbusinessangels.com.au
  At this truly amazing website you can register by answering a few questions and they will endeavour to find you an investor. The website also assists with a variety of information, such as how long it will take to find an investor, how deals are structured and how many businesses have they matched.

Grants and assistance

Grants and other funding programs are available from the federal, state and territory governments and in some cases from local councils. Generally there are few grants available for starting a business and the competition is fierce. They are often only available for specific circumstances. However, there are grants and other assistance packages available for business activities such as expanding your business, research and development, innovation and exporting.

Here are a few relevant things you should understand about applying for a grant:

- The application process can be lengthy.
- Be sure to provide complete and accurate information in the application. An incomplete application may not be accepted or can add delay to approving your grant.
- Imagine that you are about to apply for a job that you've always dreamt about and you have to create an amazing resume — your grant application will be very similar. Make sure that it stands out from the many other applications that will be submitted. Demonstrate a clear and concise understanding of your business and where it's heading. Also make sure that you clearly show where the money will be used and for what. Don't be scared to go into as much detail as possible. This grant application is not that dissimilar to applying for a bank loan (and they aren't easy to obtain either).
- Involve outside experts, if you know any. An accountant or consultant can add credibility to your application.
- Make sure that you've exhausted all of your options before applying for a small business grant. They are not easy to obtain and it may take some time for the outcome of your application to be known.

For further assistance, simply visit www.business.gov.au.

Two VIPs — your bookkeeper and accountant

Bookkeeping is the recording of financial transactions. Transactions include sales, purchases, income and payments by an individual or organisation. If you find your business has grown to the point where it is difficult to find the time to keep your 'books' consistent or to get your BAS done on time, hiring the assistance of a bookkeeper is a positive move for you and your sanity.

Useful websites:

- **www.bookeeper.com.au**
- **www.firstclassaccounts.com.au First Class Accounts is Australia's largest business bookkeeping service, helping small- and medium-sized businesses to work smarter and grow faster.**
- **www.businessinmind.com.au**

When you are first starting out in business, you are literally looking at every cent that walks out the door. As it gets closer to start-up day, the funds may be looking a little worse for wear, so avoid any unnecessary spending like the plague. This is where the advice and services of a bookkeeper or an accountant can come in handy. If you have accountant or bookkeeper friends to help you for free, then lucky you! If you aren't as fortunate, factor their services into your budget right from the start. If you're reasonably confident about doing your own bookkeeping and feel you can accurately track where your money is going, then a computer program may be all you need. Do keep in mind that unless you are entering all of your business data correctly and efficiently, you may do more harm than good. Bookkeepers are not necessarily accountants, but they will keep things thoroughly organised, which in turn, is comforting for you.

An accountant is someone who keeps and inspects financial accounts.

    Useful websites:

- **www.business-accountants.com.au**
- **www.truelocal.com.au**
- **yellowpages.com.au**

Cash is queen

Cash flow is the movement of cash into or out of a business, project or financial product. It is usually measured during a specified period of time.

I hate to be the bearer of bad news, but when you are out of money, chances are you'll be out of business. Having a healthy bank balance is critical to a successful business and this means that you need to be on top of things right from the word go. Keep the cash flowing into your business because this is the key to strength, stability and growth. Besides the fact that you will find it difficult (if not impossible) to operate without the required daily cash flow, it may also have quite a detrimental effect on your staff. A lack of cash can mean a drop in consistency and quality within the normal standards of the workplace. This may result in employees becoming disgruntled and less enthusiastic about turning up to work. The flow-on effect is that customer service suffers and your goodwill could take a tumble.

A cash-flow statement shows the flow of cash in and cash out of the business. The statement captures both the current operating results and the accompanying changes in the balance sheet. As an analytical tool, the statement of cash flows is useful in determining the short-term viability of a company, particularly its ability to pay bills.

Buying a business

Before you buy any business, you should consult with your accountant and solicitor to consider your business structure. There are asset protection issues and taxation considerations that need to be addressed. Some of the possible structures include sole trader, company, partnership, trust, or a combination of a company and trust structure.

Each type of structure attracts different set-up costs, ongoing compliance costs, tax rates and personal risk. You should also be aware that adopting a company structure imposes numerous duties on the directors of that company. You should discuss those responsibilities with your solicitor. Refer to the information given on p. 301.

Due diligence

Due diligence is the duty an investor has to thoroughly investigate a company before they sign a contract to purchase it. It would be nice to think that the majority of people in business these days are honest, but regardless of this, it's still in your best interests to perform 'due diligence' on the business that you are proposing to buy. You should do your homework and undertake extensive research before investing in any business. Research should include obtaining information regarding the following:

- the business owner's reputation in the marketplace;
- any current or threatened legal proceedings against the business owner;
- historical trading information and financial reports in respect of the business;
- the lease for the premises. The lease also needs to be assessed by your advisors. You should obtain any local government council permits or licences.

Buying a business is a serious undertaking and careful planning in terms of due diligence, financial budgeting and a detailed business plan (including an exit strategy) are critical to ensuring that you make the right decision.

Things you should check

- **The current reputation of the business** Checking with existing customers may be difficult, especially if it's a retail store. This is a little bit easier for suppliers and credit reference associations. Simply call a few of their current suppliers and ask about their credit history.

- **The paperwork** You should include conducting company searches and business name searches to verify the business and owners. This search can be done on the internet or by your legal advisor.
- **A list of employees** This should include full salary and entitlements so that you can verify the employment costs against the financial accounts. When you are initially researching the business, they should provide you with the previous three years' financial records, which will include all the details in relation to wages. Make sure you find out as much information about the existing employees as possible. This will be well worth the time, whether they are going to stay on in the business or not.
- **A list of intellectual property** Make sure it includes all trademarks, patents, brand names, logos, etc. and verify ownership of these.
- **All permits and licences are transferable** Check with the relevant authorities that permits or licensing obligations are in place on the premises.
- **Does existing stock include all of the stock up until the end of the previous or current financial year?** If you are buying at a particular time of year when big sales are on, will the stock be counted before or after the sale? This is something you will need to consider, especially if you are taking over the business after the owners have a big mid-year or end-of-year sale. The last thing you want to find out is that you have paid $100,000 for stock only to find $15,000 is left when you take it over. This will inevitably put you under financial stress because you'll have to re-build the store with stock. Goodbye cash flow!

- **Are there any plans for redevelopments or upgrading of roads expected to affect your business?** This is really important, especially if it's the primary reason why the owners are selling (but they forget to mention it). Your local council will be able to provide you with information about any future developments to your property.

- **The financial accounts for the previous three financial years** How realistic are historical costs as a percentage of sales? Would your cost structure differ greatly?

- **Customer lists** Try to determine the strength of the relationship between the customers and the business. If their lists and databases are up to date, you will have a greater insight and understanding into your future clientele.

- **Material contracts** Determine whether those contracts can be transferred to you. Remember, you will inherit all current contracts, licences and permits, and all of this must be transferred over into your name.

- **All taxes and WorkCover premiums are up to date** The last thing you'll want to do is start your new business only to discover an outstanding WorkCover claim.

- **The draft Contract of Sale** It should include comprehensive warranties provided by the vendor and its directors as required by your advisors. This is a no-brainer — your solicitor will advise you through the previous owner's solicitor in relation to any current warranties within the business.

- **A restraint of trade clause** The Contract of Sale should include this clause, binding the vendor and its directors to not compete for a period of time and within a certain distance of the business. This is not a hard and fast legal requirement but it should be spoken about with the current owner of the business. The last thing you need when buying a business is to find out that the previous owner has opened up a similar business just up the road.

- **Approval of finance by your financier** The purchase of the business may be subject to you having your approval signed, sealed and delivered. This should be incorporated into the Contract of Sale. It's very similar to that of a residential contract.

Even though some of this may seem unnecessary or like overkill, your peace of mind will be satisfied. You can sleep a little better at night knowing that due diligence has been carried out.

My Little tips

- Estimating exactly how much money you will need is near impossible. It's always better to have more than you think you'll need.
- Stick to a set budget as much as possible.
- Invest in a good accountant — this will be money well spent.
- Cash is queen — this will help you stay afloat and will make you glad you stuck to a budget.
- When buying a business, do your research. Leave no stone unturned.

Postscript

Something very magical happened to me during the course of writing this book. It's proven to me that this crazy world of ours certainly works in very mysterious ways. Two significant and life-changing things happened to me, which directly coincided with the whole premise of this book. Not only did these two things collide, but the events unfolded uncannily within hours of each other.

First of all, I've been operating my swim school at a Westfield shopping centre in Brisbane since June 2002. In December 2007, the shopping centre managers informed me that the owners of the centre were embarking on a major redevelopment plan that would directly affect many tenants. I was one of them. My initial reaction was one of extreme concern for my little business. The possible 18-month rebuild could mean that my existing loyal and wonderful customers would go elsewhere. As the months dragged on and the closure date for the school kept being pushed back further and further, the Global Financial Crisis hit, with the owners temporarily putting the redevelopment plans on hold.

I now found myself in business limbo. I couldn't develop or make any much-needed improvements to the swim school because at any given moment my lease may have been terminated. I can't express to you in words my frustration, stress and anguish during this time. To have my flourishing school in the hands of a big multinational company was truly heartbreaking, and to see it slowly show the signs of general wear-and-tear was indeed upsetting. I was in a really difficult position; I could only do patch-up or band-aid improvements to my business because any major upgrades on my part would be money down the drain. By the time I'd secured the role as host of *The Biggest Loser*, which is filmed in Sydney, I had to temporarily hand the reins over to my brilliant managers, who were well aware they were captaining a sinking ship. On weekends when I returned to Brisbane, I would visit my school and wish that I'd been less naïve about leasing in a shopping centre and leaving myself vulnerable to possible redevelopment issues. I just imagined innocently that if the swim school ever ceased trading, it would be because I went out of business or simply didn't want to do it anymore. It didn't even cross my mind that I may be asked to leave in order for more restaurants and retail shops to be built. How ridiculously silly of me! My rose-coloured glasses have now been safely locked away.

Eventually, after what seemed like an eternity, I was given my notice and the swim school had three months to pack everything up and wind down the children's lessons. My heart was breaking into a million pieces as I gave out my last newsletter. Then my six-year-old son Kai became aware of the closure and it's a moment I'll never forget. I assumed that he knew we were going to close because I had been stressing out about it for ages. It wasn't until he overheard me talking to one of my managers about it that his little ears pricked up.

'Is the swim school closing, Mummy?' he asked, perplexed.

'Yes, sweetie ... you knew it was closing,' I replied with confusion and sadness.

'I knew it was closing, but I thought it wasn't closing for a long time,' he replied, as tears welled in his eyes.

A six-year-old couldn't possibly understand the intricacies of the entire matter. He only knew that his mum didn't want to close the swim school and neither did the staff or lovely customers. I think he always loved feeling like the 'big cheese' at the school. He was always able to help himself to the merchandise and the lolly counter, and he pretty much had free rein as the owner's son.

It really was a horrible, horrible situation to be in. I felt like I was letting down the staff, my customers, the wonderful children at the swim school and, worst of all, my son was devastated. After notifying the staff and families, it didn't take long for the vultures to circle and within days I had every swim school in the area calling me with their heartfelt condolences — oh ... *and* to ask for my customer database and the phone numbers of my swim instructors. Some owners were quite lovely, and of course my main objective was to help my staff find employment and my loyal customers another brilliant swim school. As for the database, I think I'll hold on to it. I'm not a big believer in taking money for people's personal information.

Although I was incredibly sad about the situation, I was fast coming to the realisation that life must go on. Yet here is where the downfall of one business proved to be the uncanny emergence of another.

While I was writing this book, it dawned on me how many inspirational women I knew who owned small businesses. It was my goal to interview them and gather more information to add to this book. My first stop was the lovely mother-and-daughter team that owned a local giftshop for many, many years. I really wanted to interview them, because not only did their personal situation intrigue me, but their business covered so many different aspects for my book — working with a family member, trading through the GFC, owning a small business in an area saturated with similar stores, and so on.

I started in on the interview with them — only for them to confide that they were putting the store on the market. I was literally speechless! I had so many questions, both from a 'research for my book' perspective and a 'possibly interested party' perspective. I found it really hard to contain my excitement (in stark contrast to my previous night's feelings). I fired a barrage of questions at them, the most important one being, 'Why on earth would anyone want to sell such a gorgeous store?'

I asked all my questions (see Chapter 14), but I was mindful that this was time to ask the business-related questions and not get the low-down on why they were selling. Needless to say, the ladies gave me enough information about their situation for me to fill in the blanks. When the interview was over, I sat in my car outside the store for what seemed like an eternity. Could an opportunity be knocking at an amazingly coincidental time? Was fate intervening and giving me the chance to take on something that I've only ever dreamt about? I sat there and looked longingly at the quaint Queenslander facade of the store with its welcoming window display. How could I not feel excited and hopeful? While I was giddy with excitement, I did have one major hurdle to overcome before this dream could ever be realised — convincing my husband that it was a great idea.

I'm well known among family members — and in particular with my husband — for having great 'ideas' about everything. I didn't think this was an unrealistic prospect for a future business for us. I was nicely surprised when my husband seemed quite open to 'talking' about the store when I arrived home that afternoon. The fact that he was even remotely interested was a hugely exciting turn of events! I knew he wouldn't consider anything unless he was able to wrap his head around the concept and see it from a financially viable point of view. I was secretly impressed that I'd broken down the fortress of common sense that usually protects my husband like an invisible shield. Somehow I'd found a tiny fissure that had developed into a significant crack.

Before my husband could change his mind, I quickly organised with the owner for him to visit their store and see what all my fuss was about. Within seconds of entering the premises, he turned to me and said, 'This is what you've always wanted, isn't it?'

'Most definitely. And the bonus is that it doesn't have my name on the front door and it smells like candles and not chlorine.'

'Well, I'll go home and crunch some numbers, and we'll see what comes back,' he said, just like that. I felt like Carrie Bradshaw from the first *Sex in the City* movie when Big tells her that he's bought the 'Heaven on 5th' apartment for her. Well, we weren't quite at the 'definite purchase point' yet, but it was at 'crunching the numbers' phase.

Was this really happening? I wasn't quite sure how I could feel so totally helpless one moment and so completely uplifted the next. But I was realistic. I'd already been through getting the finance organised for the swim school, so I wasn't prepared to get myself too excited in case this dream opportunity was out of my reach.

This truly was the classic example of one door closing and another opening. I somehow knew that this was just meant to happen. I do believe in luck (otherwise down-on-their-luck people wouldn't win Lotto), but I also believe that we make our own good fortune. I certainly don't see myself as a lucky person — I've also experienced my fair share of family tragedy and defeats in my swimming career —but I do know that I didn't ever sit on my hands and just wait for things to come to me. I do wholeheartedly believe that I have worked my butt off for a very long time, and the simple truth is that you have to work insanely hard, have an adventurous personality and take a little risk now and then. I'm not a risk-taker in that sense, but I dare to live out my dreams instead of just dreaming about them.

So, if you really want something, then what are you waiting for? A wise man once said to me: 'Be the driver, not the passenger.' Obviously, this means that you need to take control of your dreams and not sit back and watch the world pass you by. Be the one who dictates your own destiny.

I'm writing this on a sultry February afternoon in my office as I reflect on the past five months. The swim school sadly closed on Sunday, 19 September 2010, and it was an extremely emotional day for me. With the pool officially closed and both my staff and customers having left for the very last time, my husband, Greg, our two boys — Jacob and Kai — and I, walked around the pool and reminisced about the past eight and half years. I was totally overcome by many different emotions. I was so bitterly saddened and frustrated that I had worked so hard and tirelessly only for my business to end under circumstances that were completely out of my control. On the other hand, I was excited to be starting another small business that would once again pose new challenges and offer new experiences. But most of all, I was so proud what I had built literally from the ground up. There had been so much hard work involved, but overriding all the emotions was the undeniable fact that I'd had the wonderful opportunity to pass on my knowledge of swimming and water safety to thousands of young children. The passionate and amazing swimming instructors who had taught at The Hayley Lewis Swim School would also forever stay with me.

The swim school based at Westfield Carindale in Brisbane is now completely bulldozed, which leaves an ache in my heart. If it wasn't for my lovely new store, Coming Up Roses, the pain would be almost unbearable at what *could* have been and the many more little swimmers that may have walked through the doors.

My store is an extension of my bedroom as a little girl. I am without doubt a 'girly girl' at heart and absolutely adore most things that exude loveliness. Coming Up Roses

— based in the leafy suburb of Balmoral — five minutes from home, is the small business that I only ever dreamt about but never thought in my wildest dreams could ever be a reality. We took over the store the day after the swim school closed so there hasn't been a second for me to rest on my laurels or think about what could have been with the swim school. While swimming has, and always will play an important role in my life, my little store was always, without question, meant to be.

Dream Believe Create

Hayley

Business Jargon

ABN Australian Business Number. A unique identifier issued to business entities by the Australian Taxation Office. If you do not register then you cannot claim GST credits. More info at www.ato.gov.au.

ACCOUNTANT A professional in the field of analysing and communicating economic information for individuals or business owners.

ACCOUNTS A formal record of debits and credits relating to a person or business.

ACCOUNTS PAYABLE Money owed to suppliers/creditors.

ACCOUNTS RECEIVABLE A record of the money received by your business.

ACN Australian Company Number. A number issued by the Australian Securities and Investments Commission (ASIC) to registered companies.

ACTIVITY STATEMENT Businesses use an activity statement to report and pay a number of tax obligations, including GST, pay as you go instalments (PAYG), PAYG withholding and fringe benefits tax. Activity statements are also used by individuals who need to pay quarterly PAYG instalments.

ADVANCE (PAYMENT) A pre-payment for goods or services that may not have been officially received, but have been paid for in lieu.

ADVERTISING A non-personal form of communication intended to persuade an audience.

ADVERTORIAL An advertisement written in the form of an objective article and presented in a printed publication — usually designed to look like a legitimate and independent news story. Combination of advertising–editorial.

ASIC Australian Securities and Investments Commission.

ASSET The value of everything owned by the business.

ASX Australian Stock Exchange.

ATO Australian Taxation Office. It's always a good idea to pay them on time to avoid any extra fees.

AUDIT An official evaluation of a person, organisation, system, process, enterprise, project or product.

AWARD An award is an enforceable document containing minimum terms and conditions of employment in addition to any legislated minimum terms.

AWARD MODERNISATION The process of reviewing and rationalising awards in the national workplace relations system to create a system of 'modern awards'.

BALANCE SHEET A statement of financial position or condition; reports on a company's assets, liabilities, and ownership equity at any given point in time.

BANKRUPT A person who is judged by a court to be insolvent and whose property is taken and divided among his or her creditors under a bankruptcy law.

BAS Business Activity Statement. A single document or form stating your business tax entitlements and obligations, including the amount of GST payable and your input tax credits.

BLOG Shortened form of *weblog*. A weblog is a website that is similar to a diary or journal. Many businesses with a website have a blog attached to their home page.

BOOKKEEPING The process of recording all business transactions made by the business.

BREAK-EVEN The point at which your credits or profits equal your debts or losses.

BUSINESS NAME Name that a business trades under for commercial purposes.

CAPITAL Wealth or assets that can be invested in a business.

CAPITAL APPRECIATION An increase in the value of an asset over a period of time.

CAPITAL GAIN Profits from the gain of capital assets, such as property, shares, etc.

CASH FLOW The total amount of money transferred into and going out of a business in a given period. You need a good amount of this to keep afloat and remain stable as a small business owner.

COMPANY A commercial business.

CONTRACT An agreement between two or more parties.

COPYRIGHT The exclusive right, granted by law, given to an originator or assignee to print, perform, etc. for a certain term of years.

CORPORATION A single legal entity created as an umbrella for businesses or a group of people to trade under.

COVER NOTE A certificate issued by an insurance company stating that a policy is operative; used as a temporary measure between the commencement of cover and the issue of the policy.

CREDIT The acknowledgement of an entry of payment or value received into an account.

CREDIT RATING An assessment of credit worthiness.

CURRENT ASSETS Company assets that are liquid or can be converted to cash in less than a year.

CURRENT LIABILITIES All of the liabilities of the business that are to be settled in cash within a given operating period. A more complete definition is that current liabilities are amounts that need to be paid to creditors within 12 months.

DEBIT The recording of an entry of debt into an account; the opposite of credit. (You'll want more credit than debit!)

DEBT I dislike this word but I'll include it anyway. Debt is basically the money owed to another party. If you borrow an amount of money or buy something on credit, you have an amount of debt owing — hate that!

DEPRECIATION The gradual reduction of the value of a fixed asset.

DIRECTOR A designated person who will control the company's business. The company's constitution may set out the director's duties and functions.

DISBURSEMENTS The money paid out on a business in a settlement of obligations.

DRAWINGS Withdrawals of assets (generally meaning cash) from a business by the sole proprietor or a partner.

ENTITY A sole trader, partnership, body corporate, corporation, association or trust.

ENTREPRENEUR A person who manages or organises an enterprise, usually involving some risk.

EXPENSES The costs incurred by a business.

FINANCIAL ANALYSIS Owners and managers require financial statements to make important business decisions that affect a business's continued operations. A financial analysis is then performed on these statements to provide management with a more detailed understanding of the figures. These statements are also used as part of management's annual report to the stockholders.

FINANCIAL STATEMENT A formal record of the financial activities of a business, person or other entity.

FINANCIAL YEAR Accounting period of 12 months; from 1 July to 30 June the following year.

FIXED COSTS Business expenses that don't vary each month, for example rent/lease fees set by a contract between you and the landlord, equipment leases and any fixed salaries.

FRANCHISE A company that has created a successful business template and may offer to sell the rights to the concept to various individuals. The buyer of the rights is called the franchisee.

FREELANCER An individual who works for several different companies or businesses at once. They are not dissimilar to consultants and they are paid for their services at a set rate with no benefits attached.

GOODWILL The established reputation and value of a business entity not directly attributable to its assets and liabilities.

GROSS PROFIT What remains from sales after a company pays out the cost of goods sold; generally given as a percentage.

GST Goods and Services Tax. Tax placed upon the value of a service or item.

GST FREE Various supplies are GST free, which means there is no added tax on them, but you are still entitled to claim input tax credits for them when used for the business.

HIRE PURCHASE The legal term for a contract where a person agrees to pay for goods in instalments over time.

HTML An acronym for hypertext mark-up language. It's the programming code embedded in a website's pages that are interpreted by a browser for display on the user's computer.

INCOME Amount of money left over after expenses are deducted from the sales revenue amount.

INCOME STATEMENT Also known as profit and loss statement (or a P&L). Reports on a company's income, expenses and profits over a period of time.

INTEREST The cost for borrowing money or the payment for lending money. Usually, this is fixed as a percentage of the amount of money borrowed.

INTERNET SERVICE PROVIDER (ISP) A company that provides access to the internet.

INVESTMENT The action of investing money for profit.

INVOICE A commercial document issued by a seller to the buyer, indicating the products, quantities and agreed prices for products or services that are provided.

JOB DESCRIPTION A thoroughly detailed outline of an employee's responsibilities within the workplace.

LANDLORD Owner of a building or commercial property who receives money by charging a rental or lease fee to tenants occupying the premises. A contract should always be put in place between the landlord and tenant before trading commences.

LEASE A contract calling for the lessee (user) to pay the lessor (owner) for use of an asset or premises or building to use for business or living purposes.

LESSEE Person who holds the lease on the property. They are subject to lease termination at the will of the owner of the property.

LESSOR A person who leases property or premises.

LIABILITIES Amounts owed, for example monies owed on credit cards, loans and taxes.

LIQUID ASSETS Any item owned by the business that can be quickly sold and turned into cash.

LOAN A type of debt. Like all debts, a loan entails the redistribution of financial assets over time, between the lender and the borrower.

LOSS A negative difference between retail price and cost of production.

MARKET NICHE A segment of the market that has a current need for a product or service.

MARKET VALUE The value of a product or service that is determined by what the market will pay for it.

MARK-UP A term for the increase in the price of goods to create a profit margin for a business.

MERCHANDISE Goods that can be sold or traded.

MERCHANT NUMBER A number assigned to your company that identifies the account where money will be credited when the customer makes a purchase.

MISSION STATEMENT A vital part of your business plan, outlining the overall goals for your proposed business or company.

MORTGAGE A guarantee, by way of assignment of property, to securing the payment of a debt or an obligation.

MORTGAGEE One to whom the property is mortgaged.

MORTGAGOR One who mortgages property.

NET PROFIT The money left over after paying all expenses. A common synonym is the 'bottom line'.

NET WORTH The owner's interest in the business calculated by subtracting all of the liabilities from the assets of the business.

OVERDRAFT Occurs when withdrawals from a bank account exceed the available balance.

OVERHEADS The ongoing operating costs of running a business.

PARTNERSHIP A type of business entity in which partners (owners) share with each other the profits or losses of the business.

PAYEE The person to whom money is paid.

PAYG INSTALMENTS The amounts paid directly to the ATO to adhere to your income tax and other liabilities. Your instalments are generally paid each quarter.

PERSONAL ASSETS Any personal securities (shares), property, furnishings, electrical equipment, money in the bank and any other items you may own.

PETTY CASH A small amount of money generally used within the business for small purchases.

P&L (PROFIT AND LOSS) STATEMENT Your business statement of revenue and expenses showing the profit and losses for a certain period of time.

PROFIT A gain resulting from the employment of capital in any transaction.

PROPRIETARY LIMITED COMPANY (PTY LTD) A business that is owned by not less than two, and not more than 50 people.

RECEIPT A written acknowledgement that a specified article or sum of money has been received as an exchange for goods or services.

RETAIL When you sell directly to the customer.

RETURN Your net profit after income tax.

SALES The total value of goods sold or profits from the service provided.

SOLE TRADER A form of business in which one person owns all the assets of the business, in contrast to a partnership or a corporation.

STOCK Items that a business usually purchases at a wholesale price and then resells at a retail price.

STOCK CONTROL Understanding how much stock is needed in the store for the business to run efficiently.

SUPERANNUATION A retirement program (including pensions) in Australia. It has a compulsory element whereby employers are required by law to pay an additional amount based on a proportion of an employee's salary and wages (currently 9 per cent) into their nominated superannuation fund.

TENDER A formal written offer to carry out works outlined by the person requesting the tender.

TERM LOAN A loan for a fixed period of more than a year that is repaid in regular instalments.

TRADE SHOW Also known as a trade fair or trade expo. An exhibition organised so that companies in a specific industry can showcase and demonstrate their latest products.

TRADEMARK A legally registered symbol, word or words used to represent a company or product.

TWITTER A social networking and microblogging service, owned and operated by Twitter Inc., which enables users to send and read other users' messages.

VALUATION A valuation is a process and a set of procedures used to estimate the economic value of an owner's interest in the business.

VENDOR A supplier; anyone who provides and sells goods or services to a company.

WHOLESALE The sale of goods or merchandise, often in large quantities, to retailers and industrial, commercial, institutional or other professional business users, or to other wholesalers.

WORKERS' COMPENSATION INSURANCE Money paid in to an insurance fund by an employer to compensate for injuries received by employees as a consequence of their work.

Acknowledgements

Firstly, I would like to thank all the families and swimming teachers and staff that walked through the doors of the Hayley Lewis Swim School. Many of you have become dear friends and you will never be forgotten. The efforts of my staff were amazing and it played an integral role in the longevity and positive atmosphere of the school.

Thank you to the following people for being crucial in the development of my first book: Brian Levine and Ronia Bourke from Blinc International, my editor Helen Cooney, senior editor Lydia Papandrea at HarperCollins, and my talented sister, Joanna, for her contribution to the book cover — was there anyone else who could possibly have known what I would love? ... I don't think so. I would also like to thank the lovely girls who contributed to the book with their inspirational stories — Tracey Taylor, Dee Green, Sarah Cocker, Kylie Johnson, Larraine Bilbie and Sarah Bowe.

A big thank you also to some exceptional women who make my life easier: Michelle for everything. You are like a sister and a best friend that anyone would hope to have all rolled into one. Without you, my life would be almost impossible to organise. Marney for making me look nice for the cameras and always being there with me for hours every day and keeping me sane. Only you and I could deal with the Fez Boags!

Ronia for making me laugh non-stop. All the wonderful women at Coming Up Roses.

I would like to thank my parents for giving me the opportunity to pursue my dreams and goals in my swimming career. I have no doubt this opportunity that you allowed me to have, and sacrificed so much for, has had a positive, domino effect on many other wonderful things that have come my way over the years. Thank you Dad for always being there for me no matter what and to Mum for encouraging me to follow my dreams. I love you both very much and will forever be your Lil Blackie.

To my sister, Joanna, and brother, Adam. Both of you mean the world to me and your support for everything that I attempt to tackle is always there and I appreciate it very much. And to my sister Toni, may you be resting in peace. I will never, ever forget your ability to make me believe that anything in life was possible ... IML x.

To my wonderful boys, Jacob and Kai. Where do I possibly begin? You are my whole universe. Thank you so much for loving me like you do and making me giggle endlessly. I am so lucky to have two such sweet young boys and it is an honour to be your mum.

Last, but not least, to my husband, Greg. We have been together almost three quarters of our life and I love you more and more with each passing day. Thank you so much for always believing in me no matter what crazy idea I have. Your support and love is unquestionably the driving force for everything that I attempt to do in life. You are my life.